COMPASSIONATE LEADERSHIP

COMPASSIONATE LEADERSHIP:

Building Strong Brands Through Empathy, Connection, and Continuous Improvement

by Laura Templeton

30 SECOND SUCCESS

i/Me
PUBLISHING GROUP
INSPIRE-MOTIVATE-EMPOWER

Paperback ISBN: 979-8-9899099-2-6
E-Book ISBN: 979-8-9899099-3-3
Author: Laura Templeton
Publisher: i/Me Publishing Group
Editor & Page Design: Laura Templeton
Cover Design: Yasir Nadeem
Author Photo: Brenda Jankowski

Contents

Part I. CORE PRINCIPLES OF COMPASSIONATE LEADERSHIP

Part II. 25 PRINCIPLES OF COMPASSIONATE LEADERSHIP

Foreward by Mike Driggers, Jr.

Compassionate Leadership challenges us to look beyond traditional notions of power and influence. Laura Templeton has crafted a guide that is as inspiring as it is actionable, offering a refreshing approach to leadership rooted in values of clarity, confidence, and—above all—compassion. Her deep commitment to helping others discover and lead with their authentic selves shines through on every page, making this book an essential resource for leaders at any stage of their journey.

In this book, Laura teaches us that compassion is not a soft skill but a core competency that fuels sustainable success and fosters trust and loyalty. Throug hreal-life stories, practical insights and a series of exercises, she demonstrates that compassionate leadership can transform not only our workplaces but also our communities and relationships.

More than just a framework, *Compassionate Leadership* is a call to action. It challenges leaders to step into their roles with a sense of responsibility and humanity, creating cultures where people feel valued and empowered. Laura's message is clear: empathy and understanding are not luxuries; they're vital components of effective leadership. This book will leave you equipped with tools to lead with purpose, impact, and a spirit of genuine care.

Whether you're a seasoned executive, a business owner, or someone just beginning their leadership journey,

Compassionate Leadership will guide you to find strength in compassion and inspire you to make a meaningful difference.

Laura Templeton has gifted us with more than just words in these pages, she has provided us with a new vision for the future of leadership, one where empathy is as essential as strategy, and compassion is as powerful as any bottom line.

May this book inspire you to lead from the heart and make a lasting impact on the world around you.

With respect and admiration,

Michael Driggers, Jr.
Leadership Speaker, Top Selling Author, and Instant Authority Coach

Endorsements

"*Compassionate Leadership* is a must read for leaders and teams alike. The focus on team values, commitment to the brand, and a that a team that is committed to both the product and each other creates empathy, creating a powerful approach that goes beyond a simple sale. The work is both powerful, timely and practical. Laura Templeton's deep insights into team culture, the timely use of AI, and her ability to help team members communicate authentically and powerfully sets the stage for powerful results.

Each chapter builds in ways that resonate with a team united with a common goal.

It is a rare gift to communicate effectively, demonstrate empathy, and create results where all team members contribute their gifts and strengths. Her approach helps create teams that not only cooperate, but together synthesize new information and develop the ability to pivot quickly and commit to a positive outcome, profit and commitment toward the success of the brand." – *Dr. Lin Morel, 2023 Marquis Who's Who in America, Adviser to Leaders, Influencers, and Experts, Keynote Speaker, #1 Best-Selling Author of Beyond Lovelyville*

"Too often, leaders see empathy and results as opposing forces. *Compassionate Leadership* dismantles that myth, offering a clear roadmap for leading with both heart and strategy. As an executive coach, I see leaders struggle with this balance daily—Laura Templeton provides the practical tools they need to get it right. A must-read for those serious about building trust, engagement, and lasting impact." – *Mike O'Neill, Bench Builders Executive Coaching, Leadership Development Expert, and Get Unstuck & On Target Podcast Host*

"In *Compassionate Leadership*, Laura Templeton offers a masterclass in modern leadership with her 25 principles as the ultimate guide. From empowering employees to become brand ambassadors to navigating the complexities of embracing technology and diversity, this book delivers actionable strategies that resonate deeply. It's not just a reference guide—it's a leadership toolkit for anyone ready to inspire, connect, and lead courageously." – **Mari Carmen Pizarro, TEDx Speaker, SPARK Conference Founder, and President of Whole Leadership Systems**

"In a world where human connection is becoming increasingly rare, Laura Templeton's *Compassionate Leadership* book emerges as an easy-to-read guiding light. This book is a must-read for leaders and business owners yearning to cultivate deeply connected teams. Templeton illuminates the path to compassionate leadership with clarity, confidence, and heart.

Through insightful core principles and thought-provoking reflection questions, she empowers readers to embark on a journey of self-discovery and growth. *Compassionate Leadership* reveals how to genuinely engage employees, clarifying the profound impact of their contributions and igniting a passion within them to become true advocates for the company's brand.

This book is a timely gift, reminding us that leadership rooted in compassion is not just possible, but essential for building thriving organizations in today's world." – **Georganne Ford, Executive/Leadership Coach and Speaker, By George Coaching, LLC**

"First I must say I am biased, I consider Laura a good friend and someone I immensely respect. If leadership were a language, Laura speaks it fluently—and this book is her translation for the rest of us. *Compassionate Leadership* is the roadmap every purpose-driven leader needs. I've personally walked in the story's character Rebekah's shoes—leaning into leadership, finding my voice (although some may find that hard to believe), and learning that true success comes from connection, right community, humility, empathy, and Leveling others ■ . Laura doesn't just talk about these principles— she shows us how to live them. If you're ready to get after it, lead with heart and build something that truly matters, look no further. This book is your guide." – *L. Scott Ferguson, Level ■High Performance Mental Conditioning Coach, Speaker, and Podcast Host*

"Laura's latest book, *Compassionate Leadership*, is all about bringing more empathy and connection into leadership— because, let's be honest, business could always use a little more of that. It's got a mix of ideas, real-world examples, and reflection exercises for anyone looking to level up their leadership game. There are plenty of practical tips and food for thought on building a more compassionate workplace—in whatever style of leadership you operate from—that will impact your brand and bottom line." – *Andrea Waltz, Keynote Speaker, Trai ner, Co-Author of "Go for No!" and "When They Say No", and Founder of Courage Crafters, Inc.*

"Leadership is about connection, trust, and authentic relationships. *Compassionate Leadership* is essential for anyone who wants to lead genuinely while creating meaningful connections. Laura Templeton provides practical strategies that illustrate how clarity, confidence, and compassion are crucial for success.
This book is filled with insights that challenge how you manage teams, connect with clients, or position yourself as a thought leader. Laura emphasizes that compassion is not just a soft skill; it's a powerful advantage that enhances engagement, drives sales, and builds loyalty. If you're looking to lead, sell, and serve effectively, *Compassionate Leadership* should be on your

reading list." – *Brynne Tillman, CEO Social Sales Link and LinkedIn &Sales Navigator Trainer*

"*Compassionate Leadership* is a refreshing and powerful guide for leaders who want to make a meaningful difference. Laura Templeton's focus on clarity, confidence, and compassion is both practical and inspiring, offering a roadmap to create real impact. This is a must-read for anyone ready to lead with heart and purpose, who is looking to inspire and empower others to achieve new heights. Great job Laura, truly magnificent!" – *Marques Ogden, CEO, Ogden Ventures LLC, IAOTP Top Inspirational Athlete and Keynote Speaker 2024*

"*Compassionate Leadership* is a true guidebook for corporate and entrepreneurial leaders whose goal is to build a better, stronger business through the alignment of values, brand and people. Broken down into easy to implement principles, Laura Templeton gives the reader the opportunity for incredible transformation through incremental change." – *Emi Kirschner, Strategic Consultant and Executive Coach*

Wearing one hat as a nonprofit servant leader, I value leading by example—a core principle in *Compassionate Leadership*. The book highlights transparent communication, humility, and active listening to foster an inclusive environment where employees are trusted partners and mistakes become learning opportunities. It urges leaders to build innovative teams with clear guidelines, continuous feedback, and modern tools like AI and social media. Ultimately, the book inspires a proactive, transparent culture that challenges us to lead with heart and integrity, offering a forward-thinking blueprint for lasting, positive impact." – *Lynne Williams, Resumes & LinkedIn | Executive Director, Great Careers Network*

"*Compassionate Leadership* offers a refreshing and transformative perspective on leadership, emphasizing the power of clarity, confidence, and empathy. In a world where traditional leadership models often fall short, this book redefines success by highlighting the importance of connection and understanding. Through relatable stories, practical strategies, and actionable exercises, it provides valuable tools for leaders at every stage of their career—from emerging leaders to seasoned executives. The book encourages readers to lead with compassion, fostering trust, loyalty, and resilience within their teams, and ultimately inspiring a deeper, more meaningful life and career changing impact." – *Marissa Bloedoorn, M.Sc., DTM, CEO TCS Consulting LLC, Editor in Chief "Own It" Publishing, Executive Leadership Coach, Master of Science in* **Industrial – Organizational Psychology, Master DISC Behavior Analyst**

"Laura Templeton g oes into detail on 25 principles that will make you a more empathetic and compassionate leader. All leaders need to use these principles to make themselves better leaders and to create a more engaged and efficient team. Team chemistry is important and the leader needs to set the tone. This book is good for not only the new leader, but also experienced leaders." – **Ken Cri ppen, MBA, Corporate Leader, Football Historian, and Founder of the Football Learning Academy**

"Laura Templeton's *Compassionate Leadership* has quickly become one of my favorite books on leadership. Her focus on clarity, confidence, and compassion offers a refreshing approach to leading with purpose. This book is full of practical tools that make her vision of leadership truly accessible. I recommend it to anyone ready to lead from the heart." – **Bridget Hom, Business Life Coach & Motivational Speaker**

COMPASSIONATE LEADERSHIP 30 DAY CHALLENGE

Special **FREE** Bonus Gift for **YOU**!

Your Exclusive Companion to *Compassionate Leadership is HERE!*

Transform your leadership style one day at a time with the **30-Day Leadership Challenge**—a powerful, step-by-step guide to implementing the principles of compassionate leadership in your daily practice. This bonus resource is designed to help you build stronger connections, foster trust, and inspire your team to achieve greater success.

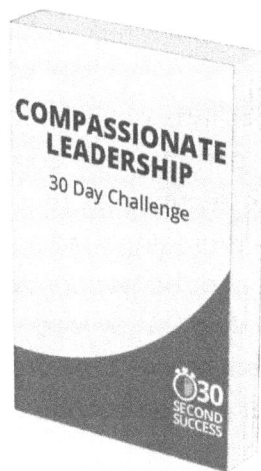

Get Your FREE e-Book And Over the Next 30 Days, You'll:

- **Master Core Leadership Principles:** Engage with daily prompts and activities that align with the book's key themes of empathy, connection, and continuous improvement.
- **Inspire Your Team:** Learn actionable strategies to foster collaboration, innovation, and purpose within your team.

- **Reflect and Grow:** Use guided exercises to deepen your understanding of compassionate leadership and identify areas for personal and professional development.
- **Build Lasting Habits:** Develop consistent practices that enhance your leadership impact over the long term.

Get your FREE e-Book HERE https://compassionate-leadership-book.com/challenge

Compassionate Leadership

"Share This Book"

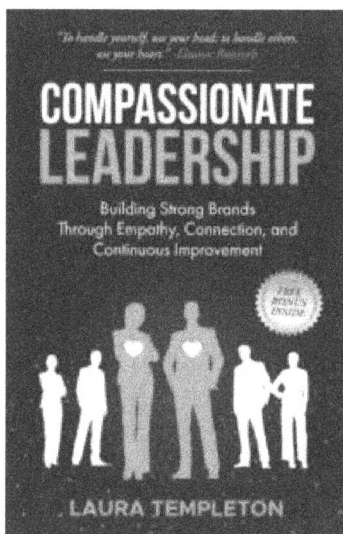

Retail $19.99 USD

Special Quantity Discounts

5-20 Books	17.99
21-99 Books	15.99
100-499 Books	13.99
500-999 Books	11.99
1000+ Books	9.99

*Price per book plus tax and shipping.

THE IDEAL PROFESSIONAL SPEAKER FOR YOUR NEXT EVENT

If your organization is committed to developing strong, effective leaders and elevating your brand's visibility, book Laura Templeton for a keynote or workshop. As a dynamic speaker and author of *Compassionate Leadership*, Laura inspires teams to lead with clarity, confidence, and connection – fostering a culture of trust, impact, and lasting success. Secure your spot today!

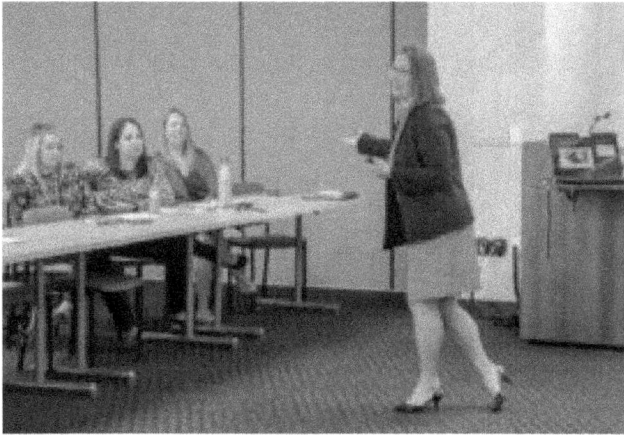

TO CONTACT OR BOOK LAURA TO SPEAK:

30 Second Success

+1 (941) 297-3311

LauraTSpeaks.com

info@30SecondSuccess.com

Dedication

This book is dedicated to you, the leaders who aspire to make a meaningful difference. To those who understand that leadership is more than just achieving results, it's about **inspiring**, **connecting**, and **uplifting others**.

To the visionaries who seek to cultivate workplaces grounded in empathy, authenticity, and purpose. To the compassionate souls who know that real success is measured not only in numbers but in the lives touched and the positive impact left behind.

May this book serve as a guide and a source of encouragement as you lead with heart, foster resilience, and create a legacy for your team and the world.

With gratitude and admiration for the
journey you are undertaking,
Laura T.

Introduction

Compassionate Leadership: Building Strong Brands Through Empathy, Connection, and Continuous Improvement

In today's fast-paced and ever-evolving business landscape, effective leadership has never been more crucial. The demands on leaders have shifted dramatically, requiring not just strategic thinking and results-driven action but also a deep understanding of human connection and emotional intelligence. The true measure of a leader lies not only in their ability to drive results but in their capacity to inspire trust, foster meaning ful connections, and cultivate a culture where authenticity and empathy are valued as essential strengths.

Compassionate Leadership: Building Strong Brands Through Empathy, Connection, and Continuous Improvement serves as a guide for leaders who aspire to make a lasting impact. It challeng es traditional, transactional models of leadership and offers a fresh perspective that places people—and their unique contributions—at the center of org anizational success. This book is for leaders who seek to transform their teams and org anizations by creating a compassionate, value-driven environment that encourges both personal growth and collective achievement.

The journey outlined in these pages delves into the **core principles of compassionate leadership**, exploring actionable strateg ies that empower leaders to build strong , resilient brands. By aligning your leadership style with these principles, you'll discover how to cultivate trust, inspire purpose, and navigate challenges with empathy and authenticity. This approach isn't just about achieving goals; it's about creating an enduring legacy of connection and positive impact.

What makes this book unique is its blend of theoretical insights and real-life application. To bring these principles to life, we follow the story of Rebekah, a young leader stepping into a new role, who learns how to navigate the complexities of leadership while staying true to her values. Through her journey, you'll gain relatable, practical insights into how compassionate leadership can be implemented in real-world scenarios.

By the end of this book, you'll be equipped with the tools, mindset, and confidence to lead with empathy and purpose, inspiring your team to reach new heights while strengthening the foundation of your brand. Together, let's explore how compassion, connection, and continuous improvement can drive lasting success for you, your team, and your organization.

How to Use This Book

For Personal Growth as a Leader:

1. Reflect on Core Principles: Each chapter introduces a principle of compassionate leadership, supported by practical examples and reflective exercises. As you read through these chapters, take the time to reflect on your own leadership style. Consider how each principle resonates with you and identify areas where you can improve.

2. Engage with Reflective Exercises: At the end of each chapter, engage with the reflective exercises. These are designed to help you internalize the concepts discussed and apply them to your personal leadership journey. Writing down your thoughts and sharing them with a trusted colleague or mentor can provide additional insights and accountability.

3. Learn from Rebekah's Journey: Follow Rebekah's story as she embraces compassionate leadership principles in her new role. Her experiences and challenges offer valuable lessons and relatable scenarios that you can learn from. Reflect on how her journey mirrors your own and what strategies you can adopt from her approach.

For Team Development:

1. Facilitate Team Workshops: Use the content and exercises in this book to facilitate workshops with your team. For example, you can replicate Rebekah's team workshop on understanding and articulating core values. This encourages collective reflection and alignment on the company's mission and values.

2. Encourage Open Dialogue: Foster a culture of transparency and open communication within your team. Use the principles discussed in the book to guide discussions on how your team can embody the brand's values in their daily work. Encourage team members to share their stories and experiences, just as Rebekah did with her team.

3. Implement Practical Strategies: Apply the practical strategies provided in each chapter to your team's workflows. For instance, introduce AI-driven tools to enhance efficiency and personalization in brand communication. Empower your team with the autonomy to make decisions and take initiative, fostering a sense of ownership and accountability.

4. Celebrate and Reflect Together: Regularly review your team's progress and celebrate small wins and milestones. Use the reflective exercises at the end of each chapter to facilitate team discussions on what's working well and what can be improved. This continuous feedback loop encourages a culture of continuous learning and improvement.

Creating a Culture of Compassionate Leadership:

1. Model Compassionate Leadership: As a leader, your actions set the tone for your organization. By consistently demonstrating empathy, authenticity, and a commitment to continuous improvement, you inspire your team to do the same.

2. Build Strong Connections: Foster a sense of connection and camaraderie within your team. Create opportunities for team members to bond and collaborate across departments. Recognize and celebrate the unique talents and contributions of each individual.

3. Commit to Continuous Improvement: Encourage a growth mindset within your team. Provide opportunities for professional development and celebrate innovative ideas. Regularly review and adjust strategies to ensure alignment with your core values and mission.

Using the 25 Principles as a Reference Guide:
Part II of this book is dedicated to 25 principles of compassionate leadership. These principles serve as a comprehensive reference guide, offering deeper insights and strategies to enhance your leadership journey. Each principle is designed to be revisited as you encounter different challenges and opportunities in your leadership role. Use these principles to refine your approach, inspire your team, and cultivate a culture of compassion and connection.

Final Thoughts
Compassionate Leadership: Building Strong Brands Through Empathy, Connection, and Continuous Improvement is more than just a guide; it's a call to action. It challenges you to embrace a leadership style that prioritizes human connection and continuous growth. By integrating the principles and strategies outlined in this book, you can transform your organization into a thriving, resilient brand that stands the test of time.

To deepen your understanding and application of these principles, consider booking a workshop for your team. These workshops provide a hands-on, interactive experience that can help you and your team internalize the concepts discussed and apply them to your unique organizational context.

Thank you for embarking on this journey with us. Your commitment to compassionate leadership has the power to create a positive impact that extends far beyond the workplace. Let's begin this transformative journey together, fostering a culture where truth, trust, and talent are encouraged and celebrated.

"Compassionate leadership is about inspiring others to see their worth, nurturing their potential, and empowering them to lead with purpose and heart."

-Laura Templeton

PART I
CORE PRINCIPLES OF COMPASSIONATE LEADERSHIP

In the ever-evolving landscape of today's business world, the need for compassionate leadership has never been more critical. The pressures and challenges that organizations face require leaders who not only drive results but also inspire, connect, and foster a culture of authenticity and empathy. Part I of this book, "Core Principles of Compassionate Leadership," lays the foundation for understanding and implementing a leadership style that prioritizes these values.

Compassionate leadership is more than a set of skills; it is a mindset and a commitment to leading with heart and integrity. It involves recognizing the humanity in each team member, valuing their unique contributions, and creating an environment where they can thrive. By embracing the core principles outlined in this section, you will be equipped to transform your leadership approach and cultivate a workplace that is resilient, innovative, and deeply connected.

In part I of this book, you will explore the essential principles that underpin compassionate leadership. Each chapter delves into a specific principle, providing theoretical insights, practical strategies, and reflective exercises to help you internalize and apply these concepts in your daily leadership practice. These principles are not just abstract ideas but actionable guides designed to enhance your effectiveness as a leader and the well-being of your team.

From leading by example and communicating transparently to fostering collaboration and promoting continuous learning, these core principles cover the key aspects of compassionate leadership. You will learn how to build trust, create connections, and inspire a sense of purpose within your team. By integrating these principles into your leadership style, you will not only improve your team's performance but also contribute to a more positive and supportive organizational culture.

Throughout this journey, you will also follow the story of Rebekah, a young leader navigating her new role. Her experiences and challenges provide real-life examples of how to apply these principles and overcome common obstacles in compassionate leadership. Rebekah's journey serves as a relatable and inspiring illustration of the transformative power of leading with empathy and connection.

As you embark on this exploration of compassionate leadership, I encourage you to approach each principle with an open mind and a willingness to reflect on your own leadership practices. Use the reflective exercises to deepen your understanding and identify areas for growth. Share your insights with your team and foster a collaborative learning environment where everyone can benefit from these principles.

Think of part I of this book as your guide to building a strong foundation for compassionate leadership. By embracing these core principles, you will be well on your way to creating a resilient, thriving organization that stands the test of time. Let's begin this transformative journey together, leading with empathy, authenticity, and a relentless commitment to continuous improvement.

1.

The Power of Leadership in Brand Building

Leadership is more than just guiding a team toward achieving goals; it's about embodying the essence of what your organization stands for and inspiring others to do the same. In the realm of brand building, leaders are the torchbearers of their organization's values and mission. They set the tone for how the brand is perceived both internally and externally. Effective leaders understand that their actions, decisions, and even their words carry the weight of the brand they represent. This chapter delves into the profound impact of leadership on brand building and how leaders can harness this power to create a unified, passionate, and motivated workforce.

The journey begins with a fundamental understanding of what leadership means in the context of brand advocacy. Unlike traditional leadership, which often focuses on operational efficiency and performance metrics, brand leadership is about fostering a deep connection between the brand and its people. This connection is built on trust, authenticity, and a shared vision. Leaders must be the living embodiment of their brand's values, demonstrating through their actions and interactions what the brand truly stands for. This authenticity inspires employees to align their own behaviors with the brand's ethos, creating a cohesive and compelling brand identity.

Consider the stories of leaders who have successfully navigated the complex terrain of brand building. For instance, Howard

Schultz of Starbucks didn't just build a coffee empire; he created a brand synonymous with community and connection. By prioritizing employee well-being and fostering an inclusive company culture, Schultz ensured that every Starbucks partner (employee) became a brand ambassador who genuinely cared about the customer experience. Such examples illustrate the transformative power of compassionate and value-driven leadership in building a strong, resonant brand.

Central to this leadership approach is the cultivation of a brand-aligned culture. This culture isn't imposed from the top down but is nurtured through transparent communication, mutual respect, and shared goals. Leaders play a crucial role in shaping this culture by modeling the behaviors and attitudes they wish to see in their teams. When leaders are transparent about their vision and inclusive in their decision-making, they build a foundation of trust. This trust encourages employees to take ownership of the brand's success, fostering a sense of pride and loyalty that extends beyond the workplace.

Leadership in brand building also involves recognizing and celebrating the unique talents within the team. Every employee brings something special to the table, and it is the leader's role to identify these talents and create opportunities for them to shine. This not only enhances individual performance but also strengthens the collective brand identity. When employees feel valued and empowered, they are more likely to go above and beyond in their roles, advocating for the brand with genuine enthusiasm and commitment.

Moreover, effective leaders understand the importance of empathy in brand advocacy. Empathy allows leaders to connect with their team members on a human level, understanding their aspirations, challenges, and motivations. This connection fosters a supportive and inclusive environment where employees feel heard and appreciated. Empathetic leadership creates a ripple effect, encouraging employees to extend the same level of care and understanding to their interactions with customers, thereby enhancing the overall brand experience.

As we delve deeper into the strategies for building a brand through leadership, it's essential to emphasize the role of continuous learning and adaptation. The business landscape is constantly evolving, and leaders must be agile and forward-thinking. They must be willing to learn from both successes and failures, adapting their strategies to meet changing market demands and customer expectations. This proactive approach ensures that the brand remains relevant and resilient in the face of challenges.

Rebekah's Story: Embracing Leadership

Rebekah sat in her small office, staring at the nameplate on her desk that now read "Marketing Team Lead." At just 28, she had worked tirelessly to prove herself at BrightEdge Marketing, known for its innovative campaigns and fast-paced environment. Her promotion came with congratulations from her peers, but also with a sense of unease. For the first time, Rebekah would be managing a team of five talented but diverse individuals, all with unique personalities and work styles. She had watched other leaders navigate through challenges with varying degrees of success, and she was determined to take a different approach—one rooted in authenticity, compassion, and purpose.

As Rebekah reflected on her journey so far, she realized that the principles she valued most—truth, trust, and talent—would have to guide her. Her goals were clear: foster

---

a team culture where everyone felt valued, encourage authentic representation of BrightEdge's brand, and deliver results that aligned with the company's vision. But she knew this wouldn't be easy. The road ahead would test her patience, challenge her resolve, and demand that she grow into a leader who led not just with strategy, but with heart.

Rebekah's first challenge arose during a team brainstorming session for a major client campaign. The energy in the room was tense; ideas were being dismissed without discussion, and some team members seemed disengaged. Rebekah observed quietly but knew she had to act.

The next morning, she called a team meeting. "I noticed our session yesterday didn't feel productive," she began. "As your leader, I take responsibility for setting the tone. I want to ensure this is a space where every idea is valued, and collaboration thrives." She shared an example from her previous role when a campaign idea she hesitated to share ended up being one of the company's most successful projects. Her vulnerability opened the floor for an honest conversation, and team members admitted they sometimes held back out of fear of judgment.

To rebuild trust, Rebekah implemented a "no idea is too small" rule for brainstorming sessions and led by actively soliciting input from quieter team members. Over time, the team saw her walking the talk—treating everyone's ideas with respect, even when they required refinement. By leading with humility and openness, Rebekah created a safe environment where creativity flourished.

Principle 1: Lead by Example

Embody the core values and behaviors you wish to see in your team. By consistently demonstrating the brand's values in your actions and decisions, you set a powerful example for your employees to follow.

Reflective Exercise:

Take some time to reflect on how you currently embody your brand's values in your daily actions and decisions. Write down specific examples of how you have demonstrated these values. Identify areas where you can improve and make a plan to enhance your alignment with the brand's values. Discuss these reflections with a trusted colleague or mentor to gain additional insights.

2.

Understanding Your Brand's Core Values

Understanding your brand's core values is the cornerstone of effective brand leadership. Core values are not just words or statements; they are the guiding principles that define your brand's identity and shape its interactions with the world. As a leader, it is crucial to deeply understand and internalize these values, ensuring they resonate authentically with your team and your customers. This chapter explores how to identify, articulate, and embody your brand's core values to foster a cohesive and inspiring brand culture.

The journey to uncovering your brand's core values begins with introspection and dialogue. Gather your leadership team and key stakeholders to reflect on what your organization truly stands for. Consider the moments when your brand has made a significant impact or when it has stood out in the market. These moments often reveal the underlying values that drive your brand. Engage in open and honest conversations, encouraging everyone to share their perspectives and insights. This collaborative approach ensures that the identified values are not only authentic but also inclusive of diverse viewpoints within your organization.

Once you have identified your core values, the next step is to articulate them clearly and compellingly. Your values should be succinct yet powerful, capturing the essence of what your brand represents. Avoid generic or vague statements; instead, focus on specific behaviors and principles that distinguish your brand. For example, instead of saying "we value integrity," you might say "we are committed to honesty and transparency in all our interactions." This level of specificity makes your values actionable and relatable, guiding your team's daily behaviors and decisions.

Embodying your brand's core values is where the true work of leadership begins. As a leader, you must be the living example of these values, demonstrating them consistently through your actions and decisions. This authenticity builds trust and credibility, inspiring your team to follow suit. It's not enough to talk about values; you must show what they look like in practice. For instance, if one of your core values is customer-centricity, prioritize listening to customer feedback, and make decisions that enhance the customer experience. When your team sees you embodying these values, they are more likely to adopt and advocate for them as well.

Creating a culture that reflects your brand's core values requires intentional effort and reinforcement. Integrate these values into your hiring practices, performance evaluations, and reward systems. Celebrate examples of team members who exemplify the values in their work and use their stories to inspire others. Regularly communicate the importance of your values through meetings, newsletters, and other internal channels. This continuous reinforcement ensures that your values remain at the forefront of everyone's mind, guiding their actions and decisions.

One of the most powerful ways to reinforce your brand's values is through storytelling. Share stories of how these values have positively impacted your customers, employees, and the community. These stories make your values tangible and relatable, illustrating their real-world impact. Encourage your team to share their own stories, creating a rich tapestry of experiences that highlight the importance of living your brand's values. This storytelling approach not only reinforces the values but also fosters a sense of connection and camaraderie within your team.

Understanding and articulating your brand's core values also involves being open to feedback and evolution. As your organization grows and the market changes, your values may need to be revisited and refined. Encourage a culture of feedback where team members feel comfortable sharing their thoughts on how well the organization is living its values. Use this feedback to make necessary adjustments, ensuring that your values remain relevant and impactful. This willingness to evolve demonstrates a commitment to continuous improvement and authenticity.

Rebekah's Story: Aligning Actions with Values

One afternoon, Rebekah invited her team to the conference room for an interactive workshop focused on BrightEdge's core values. She wasn't just interested in ensuring the team understood these values; she wanted each member to feel a personal connection to them. Starting with the company's mission and vision, Rebekah broke them down into tangible concepts, weaving in real-world examples to make the discussion relatable and engaging.

To highlight the importance of aligning actions with values, Rebekah introduced an exercise where the team analyzed recent decisions and projects through the lens of the company's principles. "How did this reflect our commitment to innovation?" she asked, pointing to a successful campaign. When discussing areas where the alignment wasn't as clear, Rebekah encouraged open dialogue without judgment, creating a space for growth and learning.

Rebekah then shared a story from earlier in her career about a challenging project where cutting corners seemed like the easiest path. Instead, her team had chosen to uphold integrity, despite the short-term inconvenience. That decision had not only solidified trust with the client but led to a long-term partnership that contributed significantly to the company's growth. Inspired by the story, the team brainstormed practical ways to incorporate BrightEdge's values into their daily work, from how they communicated with clients to how they collaborated on internal projects. By the end of the session, Rebekah's team felt reinvigorated, with a renewed sense of purpose and alignment to the brand's core values.

Principle 2: Align Actions with Values

Ensure that all decisions and actions reflect the brand's core values. This alignment builds trust and credibility both within your team and with your customers.

Reflective Exercise:

Reflect on your recent decisions and actions. How well do they align with your brand's core values? Identify any discrepancies and think about what changes you can make to better align your actions with these values. Share your reflections with your team and discuss how you can collectively improve in embodying the brand's values.

3.

Communicating Your Brand Story

Communicating your brand story is an essential aspect of building a strong and memorable brand. A compelling brand story captures the essence of your brand's values, mission, and vision, making it relatable and inspiring to both employees and customers. As a leader, your role is to craft and convey this story in a way that resonates deeply with your audience, fostering a sense of connection and loyalty. This chapter delves into the art of storytelling and provides practical strategies for effectively communicating your brand story.

At its core, a brand story is about more than just the products or services you offer; it's about the impact you want to make in the world. Begin by reflecting on the origins of your brand: What inspired its creation? What challenges did you overcome to get where you are today? These foundational elements add depth and authenticity to your story. Share anecdotes and personal experiences that hig hlig hthe passion and perseverance behind your brand. This human element makes your story relatable and eng ag ing, drawing people in and making them feel a part of your journey.

To craft a compelling brand story, focus on the emotional connection you want to create with your audience. Emotions are powerful drivers of decision-making and loyalty. Identify the core emotions you want your brand to evoke, such as trust, joy, or inspiration. Weave these emotions into your narrative, using descriptive language and vivid imagery to bring your story to life. For example, if your brand is built on the value of compassion, share stories of how your products or services have made a positive difference in people's lives. These emotional connections foster a deeper sense of loyalty and engagement.

Another key aspect of effective storytelling is consistency. Your brand story should be consistently reflected across all touchpoints, from your website and social media channels to your marketing materials and customer interactions. This consistency reinforces your brand identity and helps build trust with your audience. As a leader, ensure that everyone in your organization understands and can articulate the brand story. Provide training and resources to help your team communicate the story consistently and authentically.

Incorporating visual elements into your brand story can enhance its impact and memorability. Visual storytelling uses images, videos, and graphics to convey your message in a more engaging and digestible format. Consider creating a brand video that captures the essence of your story, showcasing your values, mission, and the people behind your brand. Share behind-the-scenes glimpses of your team at work, customer testimonials, and highlights of community involvement. These visual elements make your story more dynamic and relatable, helping to build a stronger connection with your audience.

Leaders also play a crucial role in personalizing the brand story. Share your own experiences and insights and encourage other leaders and employees to do the same. When people hear personal stories from those within the organization, it adds credibility and authenticity to the brand narrative. Host storytelling sessions where team members can share their experiences and how they connect with the brand's values. This not only reinforces the brand story internally but also fosters a sense of community and belonging within the organization.

Effective communication of your brand story also involves active listening and engagement with your audience. Encourage feedback and dialogue, and use this input to refine and enhance your story. Social media platforms offer a great opportunity for interactive storytelling, where you can engage directly with your audience, respond to their comments, and share user-generated content. This two-way communication builds a sense of community and makes your audience feel valued and heard.

Finally, remember that your brand story is not static; it evolves as your brand grows and adapts to new challenges and opportunities. Be open to revisiting and refining your story to keep it relevant and impactful. Celebrate milestones, share new achievements, and highlight the ongoing journey of your brand. This continuous evolution keeps your story fresh and engaging, maintaining the interest and loyalty of your audience.

Rebekah's Story: Crafting a Compelling Narrative

Rebekah understood that a compelling brand story was essential not only for external perception but also for fostering a sense of unity and purpose within her team. To bring this to life, she organized a storytelling session, inviting each team member to share personal experiences or insights that connected with BrightEdge's mission. This session wasn't just about telling stories—it was about listening, learning, and appreciating the diverse perspectives that shaped their collective identity.

She emphasized the importance of transparent communication, introducing the principle that honesty and openness were the foundation of trust. Rebekah guided the team in crafting a brand narrative that didn't shy away from

---

challenges. Instead, they highlighted moments of perseverance and innovation, weaving these into the story alongside the company's triumphs. This approach made the narrative relatable and inspiring, reflecting the authenticity of the team's journey.

By the end of the session, the team felt more deeply connected to the brand and more invested in its mission. They left not only with a clearer understanding of how to share the company's story but also with a renewed sense of pride in being part of it. This exercise empowered them to communicate the brand's narrative with confidence and passion, whether they were engaging with clients, partners, or the broader public.

Principle 3: Communicate Transparently

Foster trust through open and honest communication. Transparency in your brand story builds credibility and strengthens your connection with your audience.

Reflective Exercise:

Reflect on how transparently you communicate your brand story. Are there areas where you can be more open and honest with your audience? Write down specific actions you can take to enhance transparency in your communications. Share these ideas with your team and develop a plan to implement them.

4.

Empowering Your Team as Brand Ambassadors

Empowering your team as brand ambassadors is a transformative approach that leverages the collective strength of your workforce to enhance brand perception and customer engagement. When employees believe in and advocate for your brand, they become powerful extensions of your brand's voice and values. This chapter explores strategies for empowering your team to embody and promote your brand, creating a unified and enthusiastic brand presence both inside and outside the organization.

The foundation of empowering employees as brand ambassadors begins with fostering a deep sense of belonging and purpose. When employees feel connected to the brand's mission and values, they are more likely to take pride in their work and advocate for the brand. As a leader, it's essential to communicate the importance of everyone's role in the brand's success. Highlight how their contributions make a difference, not just in terms of business outcomes, but in the impact on customers and the community. This sense of purpose motivates employees to go above and beyond in their roles, driven by a shared commitment to the brand's vision.

Training and development play a crucial role in equipping employees to become effective brand ambassadors. Provide comprehensive training programs that educate employees about the brand's history, values, and mission. Ensure they understand the key messages and tone of voice that reflect the brand's identity. Offer workshops and role-playing exercises that simulate customer interactions, allowing employees to practice communicating the brand story authentically and confidently. Continuous learning opportunities, such as webinars and online courses, can also help employees stay updated on brand initiatives and best practices.

Empowering employees also involves giving them the autonomy to make decisions and take initiative. Encourage a culture of trust where employees feel confident in their ability to represent the brand without micromanagement. This autonomy fosters a sense of ownership and accountability, making employees more invested in the brand's success. Recognize and celebrate instances where employees have taken initiative to promote the brand or improve customer experiences. This recognition reinforces positive behaviors and encourages others to follow suit.

Creating platforms for employee advocacy can further amplify their role as brand ambassadors. Encourage employees to share their experiences and insights on social media, company blogs, and internal communication channels. Provide guidelines and resources to help them create content that aligns with the brand's values and messaging. Highlight employee stories and achievements in company newsletters and on your website. This not only showcases the diverse talents within your team but also humanizes the brand, making it more relatable and authentic to your audience.

Collaboration and teamwork are also essential in building a strong network of brand ambassadors. Foster a collaborative environment where employees feel supported and inspired by their peers. Encourage cross-departmental projects and initiatives that bring together diverse perspectives and skills.

Team-building activities and social events can strengthen relationships and create a sense of camaraderie among employees. When employees feel connected to their colleagues and the brand, they are more likely to work together to promote a positive brand image.

Providing opportunities for professional growth and development is another key aspect of empowering employees. When employees see a clear path for advancement within the organization, they are more motivated to contribute to the brand's success. Offer mentorship programs, leadership development courses, and career progression plans that align with the brand's goals. Invest in employee well-being and work-life balance initiatives to ensure they feel valued and supported in their roles. A satisfied and motivated workforce is more likely to become passionate brand ambassadors.

Finally, measure and celebrate the impact of employee advocacy on brand perception and customer engagement. Use metrics such as employee engagement scores, customer satisfaction ratings, and social media reach to assess the effectiveness of your brand ambassador programs. Share these results with the team and celebrate milestones and achievements. Recognize the collective effort and individual contributions that have driven the brand's success. This celebration not only reinforces positive behaviors but also motivates employees to continue advocating for the brand.

Rebekah's Story: Empowering Autonomy

Rebekah believed in the potential of each team member to become a passionate and authentic brand ambassador. To lay the groundwork, she introduced an engaging training program that delved into BrightEdge's history, values, and mission. The sessions included interactive role-playing exercises, where team members practiced sharing the brand's story and responding to client questions. These activities boosted their confidence and equipped them to communicate the brand's message with authenticity and enthusiasm.

Beyond training, Rebekah prioritized empowering her team with autonomy. She encouraged them to take ownership of client interactions, creative decisions, and project outcomes. "I trust your expertise," she often said, giving them the freedom to experiment and innovate. This approach not only lightened her workload but also instilled a deep sense of accountability and pride within the team. Knowing that their contributions directly impacted the brand's success motivated them to excel.

Rebekah also made it a point to recognize and celebrate the team's achievements, no matter how small. When a junior designer proposed a bold concept that impressed a major client, she highlighted it during a team meeting, ensuring everyone saw the value of taking initiative. By fostering a culture of trust, recognition, and ownership, Rebekah inspired her team to not only embrace their roles but to embody the brand's values in everything they did.

Principle 4: Empower Autonomy

Give employees the freedom to make decisions and take initiative. This autonomy fosters a sense of ownership and accountability, making employees more invested in the brand's success.

5.

Leveraging Technology and AI in Brand Communication

In today's digital age, technology and AI have become indispensable tools for enhancing brand communication. Leveraging these tools can streamline internal processes, improve customer interactions, and ensure consistent brand messaging across all touchpoints. As a leader, embracing technology and AI-driven solutions can significantly elevate your brand's communication strategy, making it more efficient, personalized, and impactful. This chapter explores the various ways in which technology and AI can be integrated into your brand communication efforts to achieve these goals.

One of the most powerful applications of AI in brand communication is throug h chatbots and virtual assistants. These tools can handle a wide range of customer interactions, from answering frequently asked questions to providing personalized recommendations. By using AI-driven chatbots, brands can offer 24/7 support, ensuring that customers receive timely and accurate responses. This not only enhances customer satisfaction but also frees up human resources to focus on more complex and value-added tasks. As a leader, it's essential to invest in AI solutions that align with your brand's tone and voice, ensuring a seamless and consistent customer experience.

Personalization is another key benefit of leveraging AI in brand communication. AI alg orthms can analyze vast amounts of customer data to identify patterns and preferences, enabling brands to deliver highly personalized content and experiences. For instance, AI can tailor email marketing campaigns based on individual customer behaviors and interests, increasing engagement and conversion rates. By leveraging AI for personalization, leaders can create more meaningful and relevant interactions with customers, fostering stronger relationships and brand loyalty.

Social media is another area where technology and AI can significantly enhance brand communication. AI-powered tools can monitor social media platforms for mentions of your brand, providing real-time insights into customer sentiment and feedback. This allows brands to respond promptly to customer queries and concerns, demonstrating a commitment to customer service and engagement. Additionally, AI can identify trending topics and influencers within your industry, helping you to stay ahead of the curve and create content that resonates with your audience. As a leader, it's important to stay informed about the latest social media trends and tools, leveraging them to enhance your brand's online presence.

Content creation is another domain where technology and AI can offer substantial benefits. AI-driven tools can assist in generating high-quality content, from blog posts and social media updates to video scripts and product descriptions. These tools can analyze existing content and suggest improvements, ensuring that your brand's messaging remains consistent and engaging. Moreover, AI can help with content distribution, identifying the best times and platforms to reach your target audience. By incorporating AI into your content strategy, leaders can streamline the content creation process and ensure a steady flow of compelling and relevant material.

Internal communication is equally important in ensuring brand consistency and alignment. Technology can facilitate seamless communication within your organization, ensuring that everyone is on the same page. Collaboration tools such as Slack, Microsoft Teams, and Asana can enhance team communication and project management, fostering a more connected and efficient workplace. Additionally, AI-powered tools can analyze internal communications to identify areas for improvement, such as email response times or meeting effectiveness. As a leader, it's crucial to leverage these tools to create a transparent and collaborative work environment, where everyone feels informed and engaged.

Training and development can also benefit from the integration of technology and AI. E-learning platforms and virtual training sessions can provide employees with flexible and accessible learning opportunities. AI-driven learning management systems can personalize training programs based on individual needs and progress, ensuring that employees receive the most relevant and effective training. By investing in technology-driven training solutions, leaders can empower their teams with the knowledge and skills needed to excel in their roles and become effective brand ambassadors.

Finally, measuring the impact of your brand communication efforts is essential for continuous improvement. Technology and AI can provide valuable insights and analytics, helping you to track key performance indicators (KPIs) such as customer engagement, conversion rates, and brand sentiment. By analyzing this data, leaders can identify areas for improvement and make informed decisions to optimize their communication strategy. Regularly reviewing and adjusting your approach ensures that your brand remains relevant and competitive in a rapidly changing market.

Rebekah's Story: Embracing Technology

To elevate the team's brand communication strategy, Rebekah proposed the adoption of AI-driven tools to personalize customer interactions and streamline internal workflows. The new technology included chatbots for 24/7 customer support and algorithms designed to analyze customer data, allowing the team to tailor marketing campaigns to individual preferences. While Rebekah was excited about the potential, she quickly realized that not everyone shared her enthusiasm.

Some team members voiced concerns during the initial introduction of the tools. "Won't this make our work feel less personal?" one member asked. Others worried about the learning curve and the potential for the tools to replace human creativity. Acknowledging their reservations, Rebekah facilitated an open discussion. "Technology isn't here to replace your talents," she reassured them. "It's here to enhance what we do best—building meaningful connections and delivering exceptional results."

To address these concerns, Rebekah organized hands-on training sessions, where team members could explore the tools and see how they could complement their work. She highlighted practical benefits, such as how chatbots could handle routine customer inquiries, freeing up time for the team to focus on creative and strategic tasks. She also demonstrated how the analytics provided by AI could uncover insights they might otherwise miss, empowering them to make more informed and impactful decisions.

As the team began to see the tools in action, their skepticism gave way to curiosity and even excitement. They realized that technology didn't diminish their work—it elevated it. By adopting AI to enhance efficiency and personalization, the team was able to deliver consistent, engaging interactions with their audience while gaining more time to innovate and connect on a deeper level. Rebekah's thoughtful approach not only helped ease the transition but also reinforced the importance of embracing change to stay ahead in a competitive market.

Principle 5: Leverage Technology

Use AI and technology to enhance efficiency and personalization in brand communication. These tools can streamline processes and ensure consistent and engaging interactions with your audience.

Reflective Exercise:

Reflect on how you currently use technology and AI in your brand communication efforts. Identify areas where you can enhance efficiency and personalization using these tools. Write down specific actions you can take to integrate technology and AI more effectively. Share these ideas with your team and develop a plan to implement them.

6.

Leading Through Change and Challenges

Change is an inevitable part of any organization's journey. Whether it's adapting to market shifts, implementing new technologies, or navigating economic uncertainties, leaders must be equipped to guide their teams through periods of change and challenges. Effective leadership during these times requires resilience, empathy, and a strategic approach to maintaining brand consistency and employee engagement. This chapter explores strategies for leading through change, ensuring that your brand remains strong and your team stays motivated and aligned.

The first step in leading through change is to embrace it as an opportunity for growth and improvement. Change can be daunting, but it also presents a chance to innovate and evolve. As a leader, it's essential to adopt a positive mindset and convey this optimism to your team. Communicate the reasons behind the change and the potential benefits it brings. By framing change as a positive and necessary step towards a better future, you can reduce anxiety and resistance within your team. Encourage open dialogue and address any concerns or questions they may have, fostering a sense of transparency and trust.

Empathy is a crucial component of effective leadership during times of change. Recognize that change can be challenging and unsettling for employees. Take the time to understand their perspectives and emotions, and offer support and reassurance. Listen actively to their concerns and provide clear and consistent communication to keep them informed. Demonstrating empathy shows that you value and care about your team's well-being, which can significantly boost morale and trust. Encourage a supportive and inclusive environment where employees feel comfortable sharing their thoughts and experiences.

Strategic planning is essential for navigating change successfully. Develop a clear and comprehensive plan that outlines the steps required to implement the change, the timeline, and the roles and responsibilities of each team member. Communicate this plan clearly and ensure that everyone understands their part in the process. Regularly review and adjust the plan as needed, keeping the team informed of any updates or adjustments. This structured approach provides a sense of direction and stability, helping to mitigate uncertainty and maintain focus on the brand's goals.

Maintaining brand consistency during times of change is critical. Ensure that your core values and brand messaging remain at the forefront of all communications and decisions. Revisit and reinforce your brand's mission and vision, reminding your team of the bigger picture and the long-term goals. Use change as an opportunity to reaffirm your commitment to your brand's values and demonstrate how they guide your actions and decisions. This consistency helps to build trust and credibility, both internally and externally, during periods of transition.

Empowering your team to adapt and thrive during change is also crucial. Provide the necessary training and resources to help them navigate new processes or technologies. Encourage a culture of continuous learning and development, where employees feel supported in acquiring new skills and knowledge. Offer mentorship and coaching to help them overcome challenges and build confidence in their abilities. By investing in your team's growth, you can enhance their resilience and adaptability, ensuring that they remain engaged and motivated throughout the change process.

Celebrating small wins and milestones is an effective way to boost morale and maintain momentum during times of change. Acknowledge and reward the efforts and achievements of your team, no matter how small. This recognition not only motivates employees but also reinforces the positive aspects of the change process. Share success stories and highlight how the changes are contributing to the brand's growth and improvement. Celebrating progress helps to create a sense of accomplishment and encourages a positive attitude towards future challenges.

Leading through change also involves being prepared for setbacks and challenges. Not all change processes go smoothly, and it's important to anticipate potential obstacles and develop contingency plans. Foster a culture of resilience and problem-solving, where setbacks are seen as opportunities to learn and improve. Encourage your team to approach challenges with a solutions-oriented mindset, and provide the support and resources needed to overcome obstacles. By staying adaptable and proactive, you can navigate challenges more effectively and keep your team focused on the brand's long-term goals.

Rebekah's Story: Leading Through Change

Change was inevitable, but Rebekah knew it often brought

---

uncertainty and anxiety. When BrightEdge announced a major pivot in strategy due to shifting market trends, the news was met with mixed reactions from her team. Some worried about how the changes would impact their roles, while others expressed doubts about their ability to adapt to new expectations. "What if this fails?" one team member asked during a meeting. Another voiced concern about potential layoffs, reflecting the undercurrent of fear.

Understanding the importance of addressing these concerns, Rebekah called a team meeting to openly discuss the changes. She started by clearly communicating the reasons behind the shift, framing it as an opportunity to innovate and remain competitive. "I know this feels like a big adjustment," she acknowledged, "but this is our chance to grow and lead in our industry. Together, we'll make it work." She outlined the company's vision for the future, connecting it to the team's strengths and potential for impact. This transparency helped to ease some of the immediate anxieties.

To ensure her team felt supported, Rebekah adopted a hands-on approach. She created a strategic plan detailing the steps required to implement the changes, breaking it into manageable phases. Regular progress reviews were scheduled, providing opportunities to celebrate small wins and recalibrate where needed. She also encouraged open dialogue, inviting team members to share challenges or suggestions. By demonstrating empathy and actively listening, Rebekah built trust and fostered a sense of collaboration.

Rebekah's emphasis on celebrating milestones proved pivotal in maintaining morale. After the first successful implementation of a new campaign aligned with the strategy, she gathered the team for a small celebration. "This is a testament to your hard work and resilience," she told them. Acknowledging their efforts not only motivated the team but also reinforced a positive attitude toward future challenges. By leading with clarity, empathy, and a focus on incremental progress, Rebekah helped her team navigate the uncertainty of change and emerge stronger and more united.

Principle 6: Adapt and Evolve

Be open to change and continuously seek ways to improve. Adaptability and a proactive approach to challenges are essential for maintaining brand resilience and relevance.

Reflective Exercise:

Reflect on a recent change or challenge your organization faced. How did you navigate it? What worked well, and what could have been done differently? Write down specific actions you can take to improve your approach to leading through change. Share your reflections with your team and discuss how you can collectively enhance your adaptability and resilience.

7.

Measuring Success and Continuous Improvement

Measuring success and fostering a culture of continuous improvement are essential components of effective leadership and brand building. By regularly assessing your brand's performance and implementing strategies for ongoing development, you can ensure that your organization remains competitive, resilient, and aligned with its core values. This chapter explores the importance of setting measurable goals, tracking key performance indicators (KPIs), and fostering a mindset of continuous learning and improvement within your team.

The first step in measuring success is to establish clear and specific goals that align with your brand's mission and vision. These goals should be both aspirational and achievable, providing a roadmap for your team to follow. Consider the various aspects of your brand, such as customer satisfaction, employee engagement, market share, and financial performance. Set measurable targets for each area, ensuring that they are aligned with your overall strategic objectives. Communicate these goals clearly to your team, emphasizing their importance and how they contribute to the brand's success.

Tracking key performance indicators (KPIs) is essential for monitoring progress and identifying areas for improvement. KPIs are quantifiable measures that reflect the performance and health of your brand. Examples of KPIs include customer satisfaction scores, employee engagement surveys, sales growth, and social media engagement. Select KPIs that are relevant to your goals and provide meaningful insights into your brand's performance. Regularly review and analyze these metrics to assess your progress and identify trends or patterns that require attention.

In addition to tracking KPIs, it's important to gather qualitative feedback from various stakeholders. Conduct regular surveys and focus groups with customers, employees, and partners to gain insights into their experiences and perceptions of your brand. This qualitative data provides valuable context to the quantitative metrics and helps you understand the underlying factors driving your brand's performance. Use this feedback to identify strengths, areas for improvement, and opportunities for innovation.

Fostering a culture of continuous improvement involves encouraging a mindset of learning and development within your team. Promote the idea that there is always room for growth and that challenges are opportunities to learn and evolve. Provide regular training and development opportunities to help employees enhance their skills and stay updated on industry trends. Encourage a spirit of curiosity and experimentation, where team members feel empowered to try new approaches and share their insights. Recognize and celebrate efforts to innovate and improve, reinforcing the importance of continuous learning.

Effective leadership in continuous improvement also requires transparency and open communication. Share the results of your performance assessments and feedback with your team, highlighting both successes and areas for improvement. Create a safe and supportive environment where employees feel comfortable discussing challenges and proposing solutions. Encourage collaborative problem-solving and involve your team in developing and implementing improvement initiatives. This inclusive approach fosters a sense of ownership and accountability, motivating employees to contribute to the brand's success.

Regularly reviewing and adjusting your strategies is a critical aspect of continuous improvement. Based on the insights gained from your performance assessments and feedback, identify specific actions and initiatives to address any gaps or challenges. Develop a clear plan for implementing these improvements, including timelines, responsibilities, and resources needed. Monitor the progress of these initiatives and adjust your approach as needed to ensure they achieve the desired outcomes. This iterative process of review and adjustment ensures that your brand remains agile and responsive to changing market conditions and customer needs.

Rebekah's Story: Continuous Improvement

To foster continuous improvement, Rebekah established a clear framework that aligned the team's efforts with BrightEdge's mission. She set measurable goals for each project, focusing on key performance indicators (KPIs) such as customer satisfaction, campaign reach, and employee engagement. During weekly check-ins, the team reviewed these metrics together, discussing progress and identifying areas that needed attention. "This isn't about pointing out failures," Rebekah emphasized, "but about finding opportunities to grow and do even better."

Rebekah also encouraged her team to embrace a culture of learning and innovation. She challenged them to explore

---

new strategies, test unconventional ideas, and bring fresh perspectives to their work. "Let's see what happens when we try this approach," she often suggested, creating a safe space for experimentation. When a bold idea succeeded, such as a social media campaign that outperformed expectations, Rebekah celebrated the win with genuine enthusiasm. Conversely, when things didn't go as planned, she facilitated a constructive review, asking, "What can we take away from this experience?"

To ensure alignment and keep momentum high, Rebekah prioritized transparency in sharing results. Whether it was a glowing client testimonial or feedback indicating room for improvement, she kept the team informed. These open discussions reinforced the idea that continuous improvement was a shared responsibility, not an individual burden. By recognizing their achievements and supporting them through challenges, Rebekah inspired her team to stay motivated and committed to the brand's success. Through her leadership, she cultivated an environment where growth and innovation weren't just goals—they were part of the team's DNA.

Principle 7: Promote Continuous Learning

Encourage a culture of continuous learning and development. Embrace challenges as opportunities to grow and innovate, ensuring that your brand remains competitive and resilient.

Reflective Exercise:

Reflect on your current approach to learning and development within your team. Identify areas where you can enhance opportunities for continuous learning and innovation. Write down specific actions you can take to promote a culture of continuous improvement. Share these ideas with your team and develop a plan to implement them.

8.

Part I: Conclusion

The conclusion of part 1 of this book brings together the key insights and strategies discussed in the previous chapters, reinforcing the importance of compassionate and value-driven leadership in building a strong and resilient brand. As a leader, your role extends beyond guiding your team towards achieving business goals; it involves creating an environment where truth, trust, and talent are nurtured and celebrated. By embodying your brand's core values, fostering a culture of connection and camaraderie, and leveraging the power of technology and AI, you can empower your team to become passionate brand ambassadors and drive lasting success.

Reflecting on the journey we've taken throug h this book, it's clear that effective leadership is the cornerstone of brand building. Leaders set the tone for organizational culture, inspire their teams, and ensure that the brand's values and mission are consistently reflected in every interaction. By understanding and articulating your brand's core values, you can create a cohesive and inspiring brand identity that resonates with both employees and customers. This foundation of authenticity and trust is essential for fostering a strong and loyal brand community.

Communication is another critical aspect of effective leadership. By crafting and conveying a compelling brand story, you can create emotional connections that inspire loyalty and engagement. Consistency in messaging and the integration of visual storytelling elements enhance the impact of your brand story, making it more relatable and memorable. Leaders must also embrace technology and AI-driven solutions to streamline communication processes, personalize customer interactions, and ensure that the brand's voice is consistent across all touchpoints.

Empowering your team as brand ambassadors is a powerful strategy for enhancing brand perception and customer engagement. By fostering a sense of belonging and purpose, providing training and autonomy, and creating platforms for advocacy, leaders can create a unified and enthusiastic brand presence. Collaboration, recognition, and continuous development are key to ensuring that employees feel valued and motivated to contribute to the brand's success.

Leading through change and challenges requires resilience, empathy, and a strategic approach to maintaining brand consistency and employee engagement. By embracing change as an opportunity for growth, providing support and transparency, and celebrating progress, leaders can guide their organizations through periods of transition with confidence and optimism. This proactive and compassionate approach ensures that your brand remains strong and your team stays motivated and aligned.

Finally, measuring success and fostering continuous improvement are essential for maintaining a competitive and resilient brand. By setting clear goals, tracking KPIs, gathering feedback, and promoting a culture of learning and development, leaders can ensure that their organization remains aligned with its core values and capable of adapting to new challenges and opportunities. Transparency, collaboration, and a proactive approach to continuous improvement are key to driving lasting success.

Epilogue: Rebekah's Reflection

As Rebekah reflected on her first year in a leadership role, a profound sense of fulfillment washed over her. She had grown in ways she hadn't anticipated—navigating challenges, embracing change, and fostering a team dynamic rooted in authenticity and empathy. But what filled her with the most pride was seeing her team not only thrive individually but also come together as a cohesive, motivated force. They had become the very embodiment of the values she aspired to lead with.

Sustaining momentum had been one of her greatest challenges and accomplishments. Rebekah understood that success wasn't a static milestone but a continuous journey. By keeping her team focused on progress and celebrating even the smallest victories, she ensured they stayed energized and aligned with the company's vision. She frequently revisited the principles of compassionate leadership—authenticity, transparency, empowerment, and continuous learning—recognizing their role in maintaining the team's drive and resilience.

Rebekah's journey was a powerful testament to the impact of compassionate leadership in building not only a strong team but a resilient brand. Through her guidance, her team had evolved into passionate brand ambassadors who represented BrightEdge with pride and purpose. As she looked to the future, Rebekah felt confident that the principles they had embraced together would continue to guide their growth, fostering a culture of connection, trust, and shared success. Sustaining this momentum, she realized, was not just about achieving goals but about cultivating an environment where everyone felt inspired to keep reaching higher—together.

Principle 8: Sustain Momentum

Continuously strive to maintain energy, enthusiasm, and a forward-thinking mindset within your team. Your commitment to compassionate leadership will inspire and empower those around you.

Reflective Exercise:

Reflect on your journey as a leader and the progress you have made. Identify the principles and strategies that have been most impactful. Write down specific actions you can take to sustain momentum and continue driving positive change. Share these reflections with your team and discuss how you can collectively maintain energy and enthusiasm for your brand's vision.

PART II
25 PRINCIPLES OF COMPASSIONATE LEADERSHIP

Part II of this book is dedicated to the 25 principles of compassionate leadership. These principles serve as a comprehensive guide for leaders who aspire to create a positive, value-driven, and resilient organization. Each principle is designed to provide practical insights and strategies that can be applied in everyday leadership scenarios, helping you navigate the complexities of leading with empathy and authenticity.

How to Use the 25 Principles for Everyday Reference and Guidance:

1. Daily Reminders: Use the principles as daily reminders of the core values and behaviors that underpin compassionate leadership. Start each day by reflecting on a principle and considering how you can incorporate it into your interactions and decisions.

2. Decision-Making Framework: When faced with challenging decisions, refer to the principles to guide your thinking and actions. Consider how each option aligns with the values and behaviors outlined in the principles, ensuring that your choices reflect the ethos of compassionate leadership.

3. Team Meetings and Discussions: Integrate the principles into your team meetings and discussions. Use them as talking points to foster open dialogue, align your team's efforts, and reinforce the importance of empathy, connection, and continuous improvement in your collective work.

4. Personal Reflection and Growth: Regularly reflect on your leadership journey using the principles as a benchmark. Identify areas where you excel and areas where you can improve. Use the reflective exercises provided in each chapter to deepen your understanding and commitment to these principles.

5. Training and Development: Incorporate the principles into your leadership training and development programs. Use them as a foundation for workshops, seminars, and mentoring sessions, helping to cultivate a culture of compassionate leadership within your organization.

6. Performance Reviews: Use the principles as a framework for conducting performance reviews and providing feedback. Highlight how well team members embody these principles in their work and interactions and offer constructive suggestions for further development.

7. Crisis Management: During times of crisis or change, refer to the principles to maintain a steady, compassionate approach. Use them to guide your communication, decision-making, and support for your team, ensuring that you lead with integrity and empathy.

8. Celebrating Success: Recognize and celebrate the embodiment of these principles within your team. Acknowledge individuals and teams who demonstrate compassionate leadership, reinforcing the positive impact of their actions and inspiring others to follow suit.

A Continuous Source of Inspiration:
The 25 principles of compassionate leadership are not just theoretical concepts; they are actionable guides designed to inspire and inform your everyday leadership practice. By integrating these principles into your daily routines and strategic planning, you can create a workplace culture that prioritizes empathy, connection, and continuous improvement.

To deepen your understanding and application of these principles, consider booking a workshop for your team. These workshops provide a hands-on, interactive experience that can help you and your team internalize the concepts discussed and apply them to your unique organizational context.

By embracing and consistently applying these principles, you will not only enhance your leadership skills but also foster a thriving, resilient brand that stands the test of time. Let these principles be your guide on the journey toward compassionate leadership, creating a positive impact that extends far beyond the workplace.

Principle 1: Lead by Example

Leading by example is the cornerstone of compassionate leadership. When leaders embody the core values and behaviors they wish to see in their team, they set a powerful precedent for others to follow. This principle is not merely about

"The most powerful leadership tool you haveis your own personal example."

— Coach John Wooden

demonstrating what is expected; it is about living and breathing the values of the organization in every action and decision.

Effective leaders understand that their actions speak louder than words. They are aware that their behavior is constantly observed and mirrored by their team. By consistently demonstrating integrity, accountability, and commitment, leaders can inspire similar behaviors in their employees. This alignment between words and actions builds trust and credibility, which are essential for fostering a positive and productive work environment.

Leading by example also means being willing to take responsibility for mistakes and learn from them. Leaders who openly acknowledge their errors and show a willingness to improve set a tone of humility and continuous learning within the team. This creates a culture where employees feel safe to admit their own mistakes and take ownership of their development.

Moreover, leaders who lead by example prioritize the well-being and development of their team members. They invest time and resources in coaching, mentoring, and supporting their employees. By showing genuine care and concern for their team's growth and well-being, leaders can build strong, loyal, and motivated teams that are committed to the organization's success.

In practice, leading by example can take many forms. It can be as simple as being punctual, meeting deadlines, and maintaining a positive attitude, or as complex as navigating difficult situations with grace and integrity. Ultimately, it is about embodying the values and standards that you expect from others and consistently striving to be the best version of yourself.

Reflective Exercise:

Reflect on how you currently embody your brand's values in your daily actions and decisions. Write down specific examples of how you have demonstrated these values. Identify areas where you can improve and make a plan to enhance your alignment with the brand's values. Discuss these reflections with a trusted colleague or mentor to gain additional insights.

Principle 2: Communicate Transparently

Transparent communication is vital for building trust within a team. When leaders communicate openly and honestly, they create an environment where employees feel informed, valued, and respected. Transparent communication

"Honesty and transparency make you vulnerable. Be honest and transparent anyway."

— Mother Teresa

involves sharing information, being clear about expectations, and providing regular updates on progress and changes.

Effective transparent communication starts with openness. Leaders should be willing to share both good and bad news, providing context and rationale behind decisions. This openness helps to build trust and credibility, as employees feel they are being treated as trusted partners rather than just workers. It also helps to prevent rumors and misinformation from spreading, which can create unnecessary anxiety and confusion.

Clarity is another key component of transparent communication. Leaders should ensure that their messages are clear, concise, and free from jargon. This means breaking down complex information into understandable terms and being specific about what is expected from the team. Clear communication helps to eliminate misunderstandings and ensures that everyone is on the same page.

Regular updates are also essential for maintaining transparency. Leaders should provide frequent updates on the status of projects, changes in the organization, and any other relevant information. This can be done through meetings, emails, newsletters, or other communication channels. Regular updates help to keep employees informed and engaged, reducing uncertainty and building a sense of stability.

In addition to sharing information, transparent communication also involves active listening. Leaders should encourage feedback and be open to hearing different perspectives. This means creating opportunities for employees to share their thoughts and concerns and actively seeking out their input. By listening and responding to feedback, leaders can build stronger relationships and make more informed decisions.

Finally, transparent communication requires consistency. Leaders should strive to be consistent in their messaging and actions, ensuring that their words align with their behaviors. This consistency helps to build trust and credibility, as employees know they can rely on their leaders to be honest and straightforward.

Reflective Exercise:

Reflect on how transparently you communicate with your team. Are there areas where you can be more open and honest? Write down specific actions you can take to enhance transparency in your communications. Share these ideas with your team and develop a plan to implement them.

Principle 3: Cultivate Empathy

Empathy is a fundamental component of compassionate leadership. It involves understanding and valuing the perspectives and emotions of others. Leaders who cultivate empathy create a supportive and inclusive work environment where employees feel understood,

"Could a greater miracle take place than for us to look through each other's eyes for an instant?"

— Henry David Thoreau

respected, and valued. Empathy enables leaders to connect with their team on a deeper level, fostering trust and collaboration.

Empathy begins with active listening. Leaders should make a conscious effort to listen to their team members without judgment or interruption. This means giving their full attention, asking open-ended questions, and reflecting back what they hear. Active listening helps leaders to understand the experiences and emotions of their team members, building stronger relationships and a more cohesive team.

Understanding different perspectives is also crucial for cultivating empathy. Leaders should seek to understand the diverse backgrounds, experiences, and viewpoints of their team members. This involves being open-minded and willing to see things from different angles. By appreciating the unique perspectives of their team, leaders can make more informed decisions and create a more inclusive and innovative work environment.

Valuing the emotions of others is another key aspect of empathy. Leaders should recognize and validate the feelings of their team members, showing that they care and understand. This means acknowledging their emotions, offering support, and being compassionate. Valuing emotions helps to build trust and rapport, as employees feel seen and heard.

Empathy also involves being responsive to the needs of others. Leaders should be attuned to the challenges and concerns of their team members and be willing to offer support and assistance. This can mean providing resources, offering flexibility, or simply being there to listen. By being responsive, leaders show that they genuinely care about the well-being and success of their team.

Finally, cultivating empathy requires self-awareness. Leaders should reflect on their own emotions and biases and be willing to acknowledge and address them. This self-awareness helps leaders to be more empathetic and understanding, creating a more supportive and inclusive work environment.

Reflective Exercise:

Reflect on how you currently cultivate empathy in your interactions with your team. Are there areas where you can improve? Write down specific actions you can take to enhance your empathy. Share these reflections with a trusted colleague or mentor to gain additional insights.

Principle 4: Inspire Purpose

Inspiring purpose involves connecting your team's work to the larger mission and vision of the brand. When employees understand the significance of their contributions and how they align with the organization's goals, they are more

"The greatest gift you can give someone is the belief that their work has meaning."

— Simon Sinek

motivated, engaged, and committed. This sense of purpose creates a unified and passionate workforce that strives towards a common goal.

To inspire purpose, leaders must clearly articulate the organization's mission and vision. This means communicating the broader goals and aspirations of the brand and explaining how each team member's work contributes to these objectives. By providing this context, leaders help employees see the bigger picture and understand the impact of their efforts.

Connecting individual roles to the larger mission is crucial for inspiring purpose. Leaders should take the time to explain how specific tasks and projects align with the organization's goals. This involves breaking down the mission into tangible, relatable elements that employees can see in their daily work. By making these connections, leaders help employees feel a sense of ownership and pride in their contributions.

Recognition and celebration of achievements also play a vital role in inspiring purpose. Leaders should acknowledge and celebrate the successes and milestones of their team, both big and small. This recognition reinforces the significance of their work and shows that their efforts are valued and appreciated. Celebrating achievements helps to build a positive and motivating work environment.

Leaders can also inspire purpose by sharing stories and examples of the organization's impact. This can include customer testimonials, success stories, and examples of how the brand is making a difference in the community. These stories help to illustrate the real-world impact of the team's work and create a sense of connection and pride.

Finally, leaders should create opportunities for employees to contribute to the organization's mission in meaningful ways. This can involve involving them in strategic planning, encouraging them to propose new ideas, and giving them the autonomy to take on projects that align with their passions and strengths. By empowering employees to make a difference, leaders inspire a deeper sense of purpose and commitment.

Reflective Exercise:

Reflect on how you currently inspire purpose in your team. Are there areas where you can improve? Write down specific actions you can take to enhance your efforts in connecting your team's work to the larger mission and vision of the brand. Share these reflections with your team and develop a plan to implement them.

Principle 5: Foster Collaboration

Fostering collaboration is essential for building a strong and innovative team. When employees work together and share diverse ideas, they can achieve greater results and drive the organization's success. Collaboration encourages creativity, problem-solving, and a sense of community within the team.

"Alone we can do so little; together we can do so much."

— Helen Keller

To foster collaboration, leaders should create an environment that encourages teamwork and open communication. This means setting up structures and processes that facilitate collaboration, such as regular team meetings, collaborative projects, and open workspaces. By providing opportunities for employees to work together, leaders can build a culture of collaboration and cooperation.

Encouraging the sharing of diverse ideas is crucial for fostering collaboration. Leaders should create an inclusive environment where all team members feel comfortable sharing their thoughts and perspectives. This involves actively seeking out and valuing diverse viewpoints and creating a safe space for open dialogue. By embracing diversity, leaders can tap into a wealth of ideas and insights that drive innovation and creativity.

Effective collaboration also requires clear roles and responsibilities. Leaders should ensure that each team member understands their role and how it fits into the larger project or goal. This clarity helps to prevent confusion and overlap, allowing the team to work more efficiently and effectively. Clear roles and responsibilities also help to build accountability and trust within the team.

Providing the necessary tools and resources is another key aspect of fostering collaboration. Leaders should ensure that their team has access to the tools and resources they need to collaborate effectively. This can include technology, training, and support. By providing these resources, leaders can empower their team to work together more effectively.

Recognizing and celebrating collaborative efforts is also important for fostering collaboration. Leaders should acknowledge and reward team members who demonstrate strong collaboration skills and contribute to the team's success. This recognition helps to reinforce the importance of collaboration and motivates employees to continue working together.

Reflective Exercise:

Reflect on how you currently foster collaboration within your team. Are there areas where you can improve? Write down specific actions you can take to enhance collaboration. Share these reflections with your team and develop a plan to implement them.

Principle 6: Empower Autonomy

Empowering autonomy involves giving employees the freedom to make decisions and take initiative. When employees have the autonomy to manage their work and make decisions, they feel a greater sense of ownership and accountability. This empowerment fosters creativity, innovation, and a more engaged and motivated workforce.

"Trust your team. Let them lead. Great leaders give freedom and flexibility to their team."

— Stephen M. R. Covey

To empower autonomy, leaders should trust their team members to manage their tasks and projects. This trust involves giving employees the authority to make decisions and take responsibility for their work. By trusting their team, leaders can create an environment where employees feel valued and empowered.

Providing clear goals and expectations is crucial for empowering autonomy. Leaders should ensure that employees understand the objectives and outcomes expected of them. This clarity helps to provide direction and focus, allowing employees to manage their work more effectively. Clear goals and expectations also help to build accountability and trust.

Offering support and resources is another key aspect of empowering autonomy. Leaders should provide the necessary tools, training, and resources to help employees succeed in their roles. This support can include coaching, mentoring, and access to information and technology. By providing these resources, leaders can empower their team to take initiative and make decisions.

Encouraging risk-taking and innovation is also important for empowering autonomy. Leaders should create an environment where employees feel safe to experiment and try new ideas. This involves being open to new approaches and supporting employees in their efforts to innovate. Encouraging risk-taking helps to foster a culture of creativity and continuous improvement.

Recognizing and celebrating autonomous efforts is essential for reinforcing this principle. Leaders should acknowledge and reward employees who demonstrate strong autonomy and initiative. This recognition helps to reinforce the importance of autonomy and motivates employees to continue taking ownership of their work.

Reflective Exercise:

Reflect on how much autonomy you currently have in your role. Are there areas where you can take more initiative and make decisions that align with the brand's values? Write down specific actions you can take to empower yourself. Discuss these ideas with your team and implement changes to enhance autonomy.

Principle 7: Promote Continuous Learning

Promoting continuous learning is vital for fostering a culture of growth and development within an organization. When employees have access to ongoing training and development opportunities, they can enhance their skills,

"Live as if you were to die tomorrow. Learn as if you were to live forever."

— Mahatma Gandhi

stay updated on industry trends, and contribute more effectively to the organization's success. Continuous learning encourages innovation, adaptability, and a commitment to personal and professional growth.

To promote continuous learning, leaders should provide a variety of learning opportunities for their team. This can include workshops, seminars, online courses, and on-the-job training. By offering diverse learning options, leaders can cater to different learning styles and preferences, ensuring that all employees have the opportunity to develop their skills.

Encouraging a growth mindset is crucial for promoting continuous learning. Leaders should emphasize the importance of learning and development and encourage employees to see challenges as opportunities for growth. This involves creating a culture where mistakes are viewed as learning experiences and where continuous improvement is valued. By fostering a growth mindset, leaders can motivate employees to embrace learning and strive for excellence.

Providing access to resources and information is another key aspect of promoting continuous learning. Leaders should ensure that employees have access to the tools, materials, and information they need to learn and develop. This can include books, articles, online resources, and access to industry experts. By providing these resources, leaders can empower their team to take charge of their learning.

Supporting employee development through coaching and mentoring is also important. Leaders should provide guidance and support to help employees identify their strengths, set goals, and develop their skills. This can involve regular one-on-one meetings, feedback sessions, and mentoring relationships. By offering personalized support, leaders can help employees achieve their full potential.

Recognizing and celebrating learning achievements is essential for promoting continuous learning. Leaders should acknowledge and reward employees who demonstrate a commitment to learning and development. This recognition helps to reinforce the importance of continuous learning and motivates employees to continue investing in their growth.

Reflective Exercise:

Reflect on your current approach to learning and development. Are there areas where you can enhance your skills and knowledge? Write down specific actions you can take to promote continuous learning. Share these reflections with your team and develop a plan to implement them.

Principle 8: Celebrate Diversity

Celebrating diversity is essential for building a strong and inclusive team. When leaders embrace and celebrate the unique talents, backgrounds, and perspectives of their team members, they create a richer and more innovative work environment. Diversity fosters creativity, enhances problem-solving, and drives the organization's success.

"Diversity is not about how we differ. Diversity is about embracing one another's uniqueness."

— Ola Joseph

To celebrate diversity, leaders should actively seek out and value diverse perspectives. This involves creating an inclusive environment where all team members feel comfortable sharing their thoughts and ideas. By embracing diversity, leaders can tap into a wealth of ideas and insights that drive innovation and creativity.

Creating opportunities for diverse voices to be heard is crucial for celebrating diversity. Leaders should ensure that all team members have a platform to share their perspectives and contribute to decision-making. This can include diverse representation on committees, inclusive team meetings, and open forums for discussion. By giving everyone a voice, leaders can create a more inclusive and equitable work environment.

Providing training and education on diversity and inclusion is another key aspect of celebrating diversity. Leaders should offer workshops, seminars, and resources that help employees understand and appreciate diversity. This can include training on cultural competence, unconscious bias, and inclusive practices. By educating their team, leaders can create a more inclusive and respectful work environment.

Recognizing and celebrating the unique talents and contributions of team members is essential for fostering a culture of diversity. Leaders should acknowledge and reward employees who demonstrate strong collaboration skills and contribute to the team's success. This recognition helps to reinforce the importance of diversity and motivates employees to continue working together.

Creating a culture of respect and inclusion is also important for celebrating diversity. Leaders should promote respect and understanding among team members and address any instances of discrimination or bias. This involves setting clear expectations for behavior, providing support for those who experience discrimination, and fostering an environment where everyone feels valued and included.

Reflective Exercise:

Reflect on how you currently celebrate diversity within your team. Are there areas where you can improve? Write down specific actions you can take to enhance diversity and inclusion. Share these reflections with your team and develop a plan to implement them.

Principle 9: Recognize and Reward

Recognizing and rewarding individual and team achievements is essential for motivating and engaging employees. When leaders acknowledge and celebrate the successes of their team, they reinforce positive behaviors, build morale, and

"The way to develop the best that is in a person is by appreciation and encouragement."

— Charles Schwab

foster a culture of excellence. Recognition and rewards show employees that their efforts are valued and appreciated, leading to increased motivation and commitment.

To recognize and reward effectively, leaders should provide timely and specific feedback. This means acknowledging achievements as they happen and providing detailed praise that highlights the specific actions and behaviors that led to success. Timely and specific feedback helps employees understand what they did well and encourages them to continue performing at a high level.

Creating a variety of recognition and reward programs is crucial for engaging employees. Leaders should offer both formal and informal recognition, such as employee of the month awards, shout-outs in team meetings, and personalized thank-you notes. By providing diverse recognition options, leaders can cater to different preferences and make recognition more meaningful.

Involving the team in the recognition process is also important.

Leaders should encourage employees to recognize and celebrate the achievements of their colleagues. This can include peer-to-peer recognition programs, team celebrations, and collaborative awards. Involving the team helps to build a sense of community and fosters a culture of mutual appreciation.

Providing meaningful rewards is essential for motivating employees. Leaders should offer rewards that are valued by their team members, such as bonuses, gift cards, extra time off, or professional development opportunities. Meaningful rewards show employees that their efforts are appreciated and motivate them to continue striving for excellence.

Creating a culture of continuous recognition and reward is also important. Leaders should make recognition and rewards a regular part of their interactions with their team. This involves embedding recognition into daily routines, celebrating both small and large achievements, and continuously looking for opportunities to acknowledge and reward success.

Reflective Exercise:

Reflect on how you currently recognize and reward the achievements of your team. Are there areas where you can improve? Write down specific actions you can take to enhance your recognition and reward efforts. Share these reflections with your team and develop a plan to implement them.

Principle 10: Maintain Consistency

Maintaining consistency in messaging and behaviors that align with your brand values is essential for building trust and credibility. Consistency ensures that employees and customers have a clear understanding of

"Consistency is what transforms average into excellence."

— Tony Robbins

what your brand stands for and can rely on your organization to uphold its values in every interaction. This principle is crucial for fostering a cohesive and trustworthy brand identity.

To maintain consistency, leaders should ensure that their messaging aligns with the brand's core values. This means communicating the same messages across all channels, from internal communications to marketing materials. Consistent messaging helps to reinforce the brand's values and ensures that everyone is on the same page.

Clear guidelines and standards are essential for maintaining consistency. Leaders should establish clear guidelines for communication, behavior, and decision-making that align with the brand's values. These guidelines should be communicated to all team members and regularly reviewed to ensure they remain relevant and effective.

Regular training and reinforcement are also crucial for maintaining consistency. Leaders should provide ongoing training to ensure that employees understand and adhere to the brand's values and standards. This can include workshops, seminars, and online courses. Regular reinforcement helps to keep the brand's values top of mind and ensures that employees continue to uphold them in their daily work.

Monitoring and feedback are important for maintaining consistency. Leaders should regularly monitor communications and behaviors to ensure they align with the brand's values. This can include reviewing emails, social media posts, and customer interactions. Providing feedback and guidance helps to address any inconsistencies and reinforces the importance of maintaining alignment with the brand's values.

Recognizing and celebrating consistent behaviors is also essential. Leaders should acknowledge and reward employees who consistently demonstrate the brand's values in their actions and communications. This recognition helps to reinforce the importance of consistency and motivates employees to uphold the brand's values.

Reflective Exercise:

Reflect on how you currently maintain consistency in messaging and behaviors. Are there areas where you can improve? Write down specific actions you can take to enhance consistency. Share these reflections with your team and develop a plan to implement them.

Principle 11: Encourage Innovation

Encouraging innovation is essential for fostering a culture of creativity and continuous improvement within an organization. When leaders create a safe environment for experimenting and trying new ideas, they empower

"Innovation distinguishes between a leader and a follower."

— Steve Jobs

their team to think outside the box, take risks, and drive the organization's success. Innovation is the key to staying competitive, adapting to changing market conditions, and continuously improving products, services, and processes.

To encourage innovation, leaders should create a culture that values creativity and experimentation. This means promoting a mindset that sees challenges as opportunities for innovation and encourages employees to explore new ideas. Leaders should emphasize the importance of innovation in achieving the organization's goals and create an environment where employees feel safe to take risks.

Providing the necessary resources and support is crucial for encouraging innovation. Leaders should ensure that employees have access to the tools, technology, and information they need to innovate. This can include providing access to research and development resources, investing in new technologies, and offering training and development opportunities. By providing these resources, leaders can empower their team to explore new ideas and drive innovation.

Creating opportunities for collaboration and cross-functional teamwork is also important for fostering innovation. Leaders should encourage employees from different departments and backgrounds to work together and share ideas. This can include setting up innovation teams, holding brainstorming sessions, and creating forums for idea-sharing. Collaboration helps to bring diverse perspectives and ideas to the table, leading to more innovative solutions.

Recognizing and celebrating innovative efforts is essential for reinforcing this principle. Leaders should acknowledge and reward employees who demonstrate strong innovation skills and contribute to the organization's success. This recognition helps to reinforce the importance of innovation and motivates employees to continue exploring new ideas.

Providing a framework for evaluating and implementing new ideas is also crucial. Leaders should establish a clear process for evaluating the feasibility and potential impact of new ideas and for implementing them if they show promise. This framework helps to ensure that innovative ideas are taken seriously and can be developed and implemented.

Reflective Exercise:

Reflect on how you currently encourage innovation within your team. Are there areas where you can improve? Write down specific actions you can take to enhance innovation. Share these reflections with your team and develop a plan to implement them.

Principle 12: Adapt and Evolve

Adapting and evolving is essential for maintaining brand resilience and relevance in a constantly changing business environment. When leaders are open to change and continuously seek ways to

"The measure of intelligence is the ability to change."

— Albert Einstein

improve, they ensure that their organization remains agile, innovative, and competitive. This principle is crucial for navigating challenges, seizing opportunities, and driving long-term success.

To adapt and evolve, leaders should foster a culture of continuous improvement. This means encouraging employees to seek out new ways of doing things, learn from their experiences, and strive for excellence. Leaders should emphasize the importance of adaptability and continuous improvement in achieving the organization's goals and create an environment where employees feel empowered to innovate and evolve.

Providing the necessary resources and support is crucial for adapting and evolving. Leaders should ensure that employees have access to the tools, technology, and information they need to adapt to new challenges and opportunities. This can include providing access to research and development resources, investing in new technologies, and offering training and development opportunities. By providing these resources, leaders can empower their team to adapt and evolve.

Creating opportunities for collaboration and cross-functional teamwork is also important for fostering adaptability and evolution. Leaders should encourage employees from different departments and backgrounds to work together and share ideas. This can include setting up innovation teams, holding brainstorming sessions, and creating forums for idea-sharing. Collaboration helps to bring diverse perspectives and ideas to the table, leading to more innovative solutions.

Recognizing and celebrating adaptability and continuous improvement is essential for reinforcing this principle. Leaders should acknowledge and reward employees who demonstrate strong adaptability and contribute to the organization's success. This recognition helps to reinforce the importance of adaptability and motivates employees to continue seeking ways to improve.

Providing a framework for evaluating and implementing new ideas is also crucial. Leaders should establish a clear process for evaluating the feasibility and potential impact of new ideas and for implementing them if they show promise. This framework helps to ensure that innovative ideas are taken seriously and can be developed and implemented.

Reflective Exercise:

Reflect on how you currently adapt and evolve within your team. Are there areas where you can improve? Write down specific actions you can take to enhance adaptability and continuous improvement. Share these reflections with your team and develop a plan to implement them.

Principle 13: Prioritize Well-being

Prioritizing the physical, mental, and emotional well-being of your team is essential for fostering a positive and productive work environment. When leaders support their team's well-being, they create a culture of care and respect, leading to

"Take care of your employees and they'll take care of your business."

— Richard Branson

increased engagement, motivation, and overall job satisfaction. This principle is crucial for building a resilient and high-performing team.

To prioritize well-being, leaders should create a supportive work environment that values and promotes well-being. This means implementing policies and practices that support work-life balance, such as flexible working hours, remote work options, and generous leave policies. Leaders should also encourage employees to take breaks, use their vacation time, and avoid burnout.

Providing access to well-being resources and support is crucial for promoting well-being. Leaders should ensure that employees have access to resources and support for their physical, mental, and emotional health. This can include offering wellness programs, providing access to mental health services, and promoting healthy lifestyle choices. By providing these resources, leaders can empower their team to take charge of their well-being.

Encouraging open communication about well-being is also important. Leaders should create an environment where employees feel comfortable discussing their well-being and seeking support when needed. This involves being approachable, listening to employees' concerns, and offering support and guidance. By fostering open communication, leaders can build trust and create a culture of care and respect.

Recognizing and celebrating well-being efforts is essential for reinforcing this principle. Leaders should acknowledge and reward employees who prioritize their well-being and contribute to a positive work environment. This recognition helps to reinforce the importance of well-being and motivates employees to continue prioritizing their health and happiness.

Providing opportunities for well-being activities is also important. Leaders should create opportunities for employees to engage in well-being activities, such as team-building exercises, wellness challenges, and mindfulness sessions. By offering these opportunities, leaders can promote a culture of well-being and create a more positive and supportive work environment.

Reflective Exercise:

Reflect on how you currently prioritize well-being within your team. Are there areas where you can improve? Write down specific actions you can take to enhance well-being. Share these reflections with your team and develop a plan to implement them.

Principle 14: Listen Actively

Active listening is a crucial component of effective leadership. When leaders pay attention to feedback and act on it, they build trust, foster open communication, and create a culture of continuous improvement. Active listening involves not only hearing what is being said but also understanding and valuing the perspectives and emotions of others.

"The most basic of all human needs is the need to understand and be understood. The best way to understand people is to listen to them."

— Ralph Nichols

To listen actively, leaders should make a conscious effort to be fully present during conversations. This means setting aside distractions, making eye contact, and focusing on the speaker. By being fully present, leaders show that they value and respect the speaker's input, building trust and rapport.

Asking open-ended questions is also important for active listening. Leaders should ask questions that encourage the speaker to share more information and provide deeper insights. This can include questions like "Can you tell me more about that?" or "How did that make you feel?" Open-ended questions help to facilitate meaningful dialogue and encourage the sharing of diverse perspectives.

Reflecting back what is heard is another key aspect of active listening. Leaders should summarize and paraphrase what the speaker has said to ensure they have understood correctly. This can include statements like "So what I'm hearing is..." or "It sounds like you're saying..." Reflecting back helps to clarify understanding and shows that the leader is engaged and attentive.

Being empathetic and validating the speaker's emotions is crucial for active listening. Leaders should acknowledge and validate the speaker's feelings, showing that they understand and care. This can include statements like "I can see how that would be frustrating" or "It sounds like that was really challenging for you." Validating emotions helps to build trust and create a supportive environment.

Acting on feedback is essential for reinforcing active listening. Leaders should take the feedback they receive seriously and make changes based on the input. This can include implementing new ideas, addressing concerns, and providing follow-up. By acting on feedback, leaders show that they value and respect the input of their team, building trust and fostering a culture of continuous improvement.

Reflective Exercise:

Reflect on how you currently listen actively within your team. Are there areas where you can improve? Write down specific actions you can take to enhance your active listening skills. Share these reflections with your team and develop a plan to implement them.

Principle 15: Build Trust

Building trust is essential for effective leadership and a strong team. Trust is the foundation of all successful relationships and is crucial for fostering collaboration, engagement, and a positive work environment. When leaders establish and maintain trust through integrity and reliability, they create a culture of transparency and mutual respect.

"Trust is the glue of life. It's the most essential ingredient in effective communication. It's the foundational principle that holds all relationships."

— Stephen R. Covey

To build trust, leaders should demonstrate integrity in their actions and decisions. This means being honest, ethical, and consistent in all interactions. Leaders should keep their promises, admit their mistakes, and act in the best interests of their team and organization. By demonstrating integrity, leaders build credibility and earn the trust of their team.

Being reliable and dependable is crucial for building trust. Leaders should consistently follow through on their commitments and be accountable for their actions. This means being punctual, meeting deadlines, and delivering on promises. Reliability shows that leaders are dependable and can be trusted to fulfill their responsibilities.

Open and transparent communication is essential for building trust. Leaders should share information openly and honestly, providing context and rationale behind decisions. This includes being transparent about both successes and challenges and involving the team in decision-making processes. Open communication helps to build trust and create a culture of transparency and mutual respect.

Showing empathy and understanding is also important for building trust. Leaders should take the time to understand the perspectives and emotions of their team members and show genuine care and concern. This involves actively listening, validating feelings, and offering support. By showing empathy, leaders build strong relationships and create a supportive work environment.

Recognizing and celebrating trust-building behaviors is essential for reinforcing this principle. Leaders should acknowledge and reward employees who demonstrate integrity, reliability, and transparency. This recognition helps to reinforce the importance of trust and motivates employees to continue building and maintaining trust within the team.

Reflective Exercise:

Reflect on how you currently build trust within your team. Are there areas where you can improve? Write down specific actions you can take to enhance trust. Share these reflections with your team and develop a plan to implement them.

Principle 16: Create Connections

Creating connections is essential for building a strong and cohesive team. When leaders foster a sense of community and belonging within their team, they create a supportive and collaborative work environment. This principle is crucial for enhancing engagement, motivation, and overall job satisfaction.

"Connection is why we're here; it is what gives purpose and meaning to our lives."

— Brené Brown

To create connections, leaders should encourage open communication and collaboration within the team. This means creating opportunities for team members to interact, share ideas, and work together. Leaders should facilitate regular team meetings, brainstorming sessions, and social events that promote interaction and collaboration.

Building relationships based on trust and mutual respect is crucial for creating connections. Leaders should take the time to get to know their team members on a personal level, understanding their strengths, interests, and aspirations. By building strong relationships, leaders create a sense of community and foster a supportive work environment.

Encouraging teamwork and collaboration is also important for creating connections. Leaders should promote a culture of teamwork where team members feel comfortable working together and supporting each other. This involves setting clear team goals, recognizing collaborative efforts, and creating opportunities for cross-functional teamwork.

Providing opportunities for team-building activities is essential for fostering connections. Leaders should organize team-building exercises, retreats, and social events that allow team members to bond and build relationships. These activities help to create a sense of camaraderie and strengthen the team's cohesion.

Recognizing and celebrating team achievements is crucial for reinforcing this principle. Leaders should acknowledge and reward the collective efforts and successes of the team. This recognition helps to build a sense of pride and accomplishment, motivating employees to continue working together and supporting each other.

Reflective Exercise:

Reflect on how you currently create connections within your team. Are there areas where you can improve? Write down specific actions you can take to enhance connections. Share these reflections with your team and develop a plan to implement them.

Principle 17: Focus on Impact

Focusing on impact involves measuring success by the positive impact you have on customers and the community. When leaders prioritize impact, they create a sense of purpose and drive within their team. This principle is crucial for

"The best way to find yourself is to lose yourself in the service of others."

— Mahatma Gandhi

fostering a mission-driven organization that strives to make a difference in the world.

To focus on impact, leaders should clearly define and communicate the organization's mission and vision. This means articulating the broader goals and aspirations of the brand and explaining how the team's work contributes to these objectives. By providing this context, leaders help employees understand the significance of their contributions and feel a sense of purpose.

Setting measurable goals and key performance indicators (KPIs) that align with the organization's mission is essential for focusing on impact. Leaders should establish clear and specific goals that reflect the desired impact on customers and the community. These goals should be regularly reviewed and assessed to ensure that the organization is making progress towards its mission.

Encouraging a customer-centric mindset is crucial for focusing on impact. Leaders should prioritize the needs and satisfaction of customers, ensuring that their products and services meet and exceed customer expectations. This involves actively seeking and acting on customer feedback, continuously improving products and services, and creating a positive customer experience.

Engaging with the community is also important for focusing on impact. Leaders should create opportunities for the organization to contribute to and support the community. This can include corporate social responsibility initiatives, community outreach programs, and partnerships with local organizations. By engaging with the community, leaders can create a positive impact and build a strong, mission-driven brand.

Recognizing and celebrating impact-driven achievements is essential for reinforcing this principle. Leaders should acknowledge and reward employees who contribute to the organization's mission and make a positive impact. This recognition helps to reinforce the importance of impact and motivates employees to continue striving to make a difference.

Reflective Exercise:

Reflect on how you currently focus on impact within your team. Are there areas where you can improve? Write down specific actions you can take to enhance your focus on impact. Share these reflections with your team and develop a plan to implement them.

Principle 18: Leverage Technology

Leveraging technology is essential for enhancing efficiency and personalization in brand communication. When leaders use AI and technology effectively, they can streamline internal processes, improve customer

"Technology is best when it brings people together."

— Matt Mullenweg

interactions, and ensure consistent brand messaging across all touchpoints. This principle is crucial for staying competitive and driving the organization's success in a digital age.

To leverage technology, leaders should identify and implement AI-driven tools and technologies that align with the organization's goals and values. This can include chatbots for customer support, AI algorithms for personalized marketing, and data analytics tools for tracking performance. By implementing these technologies, leaders can enhance efficiency and provide a more personalized customer experience.

Providing training and support for technology adoption is crucial for leveraging technology. Leaders should ensure that employees have the necessary skills and knowledge to use the new tools and technologies effectively. This can include offering training programs, workshops, and online courses. By providing this support, leaders can empower their team to leverage technology to its full potential.

Creating a culture of innovation and experimentation is also important for leveraging technology. Leaders should encourage employees to explore new technologies and experiment with different approaches. This involves being open to new ideas, supporting risk-taking, and providing the necessary resources for innovation. By fostering a culture of innovation, leaders can drive continuous improvement and stay ahead of the competition.

Monitoring and evaluating the effectiveness of technology initiatives is essential for leveraging technology. Leaders should regularly review the performance of AI-driven tools and technologies to ensure they are meeting the organization's goals. This can include tracking key performance indicators (KPIs), gathering feedback from employees and customers, and making data-driven decisions. By monitoring and evaluating technology initiatives, leaders can identify areas for improvement and make informed decisions.

Recognizing and celebrating technology-driven achievements is crucial for reinforcing this principle. Leaders should acknowledge and reward employees who effectively leverage technology to enhance efficiency and personalization. This recognition helps to reinforce the importance of technology and motivates employees to continue exploring new tools and technologies.

Reflective Exercise:

Reflect on how you currently leverage technology within your team. Are there areas where you can improve? Write down specific actions you can take to enhance your use of technology. Share these reflections with your team and develop a plan to implement them.

Principle 19: Share the Vision

Sharing the vision involves clearly articulating and communicating the brand's vision with the entire team. When leaders share the vision, they create a sense of direction and purpose, aligning the team's efforts towards common goals. This principle is crucial for fostering a unified and motivated workforce that is committed to achieving the organization's mission.

"A leader's job is to look into the future and see the organization not as it is, but as it can become."

— Jack Welch

To share the vision, leaders should clearly define and communicate the brand's vision and goals. This means articulating the broader aspirations of the organization and explaining how the team's work contributes to these objectives. By providing this context, leaders help employees understand the significance of their contributions and feel a sense of purpose.

Creating opportunities for team members to engage with the vision is crucial for sharing the vision. Leaders should involve employees in strategic planning, decision-making, and goal-setting processes. This can include team meetings, workshops, and brainstorming sessions. By involving employees, leaders create a sense of ownership and commitment to the vision.

Providing regular updates and progress reports is essential for sharing the vision. Leaders should keep the team informed about the organization's progress towards its goals and any changes to the vision. This can include regular team meetings, emails, and newsletters. Regular updates help to keep the vision top of mind and ensure that everyone is aligned.

Encouraging open communication and feedback is important for sharing the vision. Leaders should create an environment where employees feel comfortable sharing their thoughts and ideas about the vision. This involves actively seeking and listening to feedback, addressing concerns, and making adjustments as needed. Open communication helps to build trust and create a shared sense of purpose.

Recognizing and celebrating achievements that align with the vision is crucial for reinforcing this principle. Leaders should acknowledge and reward employees who contribute to the organization's vision and make a positive impact. This recognition helps to reinforce the importance of the vision and motivates employees to continue striving towards the organization's goals.

Reflective Exercise:

Reflect on how you currently share the vision within your team. Are there areas where you can improve? Write down specific actions you can take to enhance your communication of the vision. Share these reflections with your team and develop a plan to implement them.

Principle 20: Align Actions with Values

Aligning actions with values is essential for building trust and credibility within an organization. When leaders ensure that all decisions and actions reflect the brand's core values, they create a cohesive and trustworthy brand identity. This principle is crucial for fostering a culture of integrity and consistency.

"Values are like fingerprints. Nobody's are the same, but you leave them all over everything you do."

— Elvis Presley

To align actions with values, leaders should clearly define and communicate the organization's core values. This means articulating the guiding principles that define the brand's identity and explaining how these values should be reflected in daily actions and decisions. By providing this context, leaders help employees understand the importance of aligning their actions with the brand's values.

Creating clear guidelines and standards for behavior and decision-making is crucial for aligning actions with values. Leaders should establish guidelines that reflect the brand's values and ensure that all team members understand and adhere to them. This can include codes of conduct, decision-making frameworks, and performance evaluation criteria. Clear guidelines help to ensure consistency and accountability.

Providing regular training and reinforcement is essential for aligning actions with values. Leaders should offer ongoing training to ensure that employees understand and internalize the brand's values. This can include workshops, seminars, and online courses. Regular reinforcement helps to keep the values top of mind and ensures that employees continue to uphold them in their daily work.

Monitoring and feedback are important for aligning actions with values. Leaders should regularly review actions and decisions to ensure they align with the brand's values. This can include performance evaluations, feedback sessions, and audits. Providing feedback and guidance helps to address any misalignments and reinforces the importance of aligning actions with values.

Recognizing and celebrating value-driven behaviors is crucial for reinforcing this principle. Leaders should acknowledge and reward employees who consistently demonstrate the brand's values in their actions and decisions. This recognition helps to reinforce the importance of values and motivates employees to continue aligning their actions with the brand's principles.

Reflective Exercise:

Reflect on how you currently align actions with values within your team. Are there areas where you can improve? Write down specific actions you can take to enhance alignment. Share these reflections with your team and develop a plan to implement them.

Principle 21: Support Growth

Supporting growth involves providing opportunities for professional and personal development within the organization. When leaders invest in the growth of their team members, they create a motivated, engaged, and high-performing workforce. This principle is crucial for fostering a culture of continuous learning and improvement.

"Leaders become great, not because of their power, but because of their ability to empower others."

— John Maxwell

To support growth, leaders should provide access to a variety of development opportunities. This can include workshops, seminars, online courses, and on-the-job training. By offering diverse learning options, leaders can cater to different learning styles and preferences, ensuring that all employees have the opportunity to develop their skills.

Encouraging a growth mindset is crucial for supporting growth. Leaders should emphasize the importance of learning and development and encourage employees to see challenges as opportunities for growth. This involves creating a culture where mistakes are viewed as learning experiences and where continuous improvement is valued. By fostering a growth mindset, leaders can motivate employees to embrace learning and strive for excellence.

Providing personalized support and guidance is essential for supporting growth. Leaders should offer coaching and mentoring to help employees identify their strengths, set goals, and develop their skills. This can involve regular one-on-one meetings, feedback sessions, and mentoring relationships. By offering personalized support, leaders can help employees achieve their full potential.

Recognizing and celebrating growth and development is important for reinforcing this principle. Leaders should acknowledge and reward employees who demonstrate a commitment to learning and development. This recognition helps to reinforce the importance of growth and motivates employees to continue investing in their development.

Creating opportunities for career advancement is also crucial for supporting growth. Leaders should provide clear career progression paths and opportunities for employees to take on new challenges and responsibilities. This can include promotions, lateral moves, and special projects. By offering opportunities for career advancement, leaders can motivate employees to continue growing and developing within the organization.

Reflective Exercise:

Reflect on how you currently support growth within your team. Are there areas where you can improve? Write down specific actions you can take to enhance growth opportunities. Share these reflections with your team and develop a plan to implement them.

Principle 22: Engage Authentically

Engaging authentically involves interacting with customers and employees in a genuine and meaningful way. When leaders engage authentically, they build trust, foster strong relationships, and create a positive brand image. This principle is crucial for creating a culture of transparency and mutual respect.

"Authenticity is the daily practice of letting go of who we think we're supposed to be and embracing who we are."

— Brené Brown

To engage authentically, leaders should be genuine and honest in their interactions. This means being true to themselves and the brand's values, and avoiding pretense or manipulation. Authentic engagement involves sharing real experiences, emotions, and perspectives, and being open and honest about challenges and successes.

Creating opportunities for meaningful interactions is crucial for engaging authentically. Leaders should encourage open communication and dialogue with customers and employees. This can include regular team meetings, customer feedback sessions, and social media interactions. By creating opportunities for meaningful interactions, leaders can build strong relationships and foster a sense of community.\

Listening actively and empathetically is essential for engaging authentically. Leaders should make a conscious effort to listen to the perspectives and emotions of others and show genuine care and concern. This involves asking open-ended questions, reflecting what is heard, and validating emotions. Active listening helps to build trust and create a supportive environment.

Being responsive and acting on feedback is important for engaging authentically. Leaders should take feedback seriously and make changes based on the input. This can include implementing new ideas, addressing concerns, and providing follow-up. By being responsive, leaders show that they value and respect the input of their team and customers.

Recognizing and celebrating authentic engagement is crucial for reinforcing this principle. Leaders should acknowledge and reward employees who engage authentically with customers and colleagues. This recognition helps to reinforce the importance of authenticity and motivates employees to continue engaging in a genuine and meaningful way.

Reflective Exercise:

Reflect on how you currently engage authentically within your team. Are there areas where you can improve? Write down specific actions you can take to enhance authentic engagement. Share these reflections with your team and develop a plan to implement them.

Principle 23: Embrace Feedback

Embracing feedback involves viewing feedback as an opportunity to learn and grow. When leaders embrace feedback, they create a culture of continuous improvement and open communication. This principle is crucial for fostering a supportive and high-performing work environment.

"Feedback is the breakfast of champions."

— Ken Blanchard

To embrace feedback, leaders should actively seek out and welcome feedback from others. This means creating opportunities for employees, customers, and stakeholders to share their thoughts and perspectives. Leaders should ask for feedback regularly, through surveys, focus groups, and one-on-one meetings. By seeking feedback, leaders show that they value the input of others and are committed to continuous improvement.

Listening to and understanding feedback is crucial for embracing feedback. Leaders should make a conscious effort to listen to the feedback without judgment or defensiveness. This involves being open-minded and willing to see things from different perspectives. By understanding feedback, leaders can identify areas for improvement and make informed decisions.

Taking action on feedback is essential for reinforcing this principle. Leaders should take feedback seriously and make changes based on the input. This can include implementing new ideas, addressing concerns, and providing follow-up. By taking action on feedback, leaders show that they value and respect the input of their team and customers.

Creating a safe and supportive environment for feedback is important for embracing feedback. Leaders should foster a culture where employees feel comfortable sharing their thoughts and perspectives without fear of retribution. This involves setting clear expectations for behavior, providing support for those who share feedback, and addressing any instances of retaliation. By creating a safe environment, leaders can encourage open and honest feedback.

Recognizing and celebrating feedback-driven improvements is crucial for reinforcing this principle. Leaders should acknowledge and reward employees who contribute to feedback-driven improvements. This recognition helps to reinforce the importance of feedback and motivates employees to continue sharing their thoughts and perspectives.

Reflective Exercise:

Reflect on how you currently embrace feedback within your team. Are there areas where you can improve? Write down specific actions you can take to enhance your approach to feedback. Share these reflections with your team and develop a plan to implement them.

Principle 24: Lead with Compassion

Leading with compassion involves approaching leadership with kindness, understanding, and a focus on building positive relationships. When leaders lead with compassion, they create a supportive and inclusive work environment where employees feel valued and respected. This principle is crucial for fostering a culture of care and empathy.

"Compassionate leaders are not soft; they are courageous enough to listen with their hearts."

— Peter Boolkah

To lead with compassion, leaders should demonstrate kindness and understanding in their interactions. This means being approachable, empathetic, and willing to listen to the concerns and needs of others. Leaders should show genuine care and concern for the well-being of their team members and be willing to offer support and assistance.

Creating a supportive work environment is crucial for leading with compassion. Leaders should implement policies and practices that promote well-being, such as flexible working hours, mental health support, and wellness programs. By creating a supportive environment, leaders can ensure that employees feel valued and cared for.

Encouraging open communication and dialogue is essential for leading with compassion. Leaders should create opportunities for employees to share their thoughts and concerns and be willing to listen and respond. This involves being open to feedback, addressing concerns, and providing support. Open communication helps to build trust and create a supportive environment.

Recognizing and celebrating compassionate behaviors is important for reinforcing this principle. Leaders should acknowledge and reward employees who demonstrate kindness and empathy in their interactions. This recognition helps to reinforce the importance of compassion and motivates employees to continue leading with kindness.

Providing training and development on compassionate leadership is crucial for fostering this principle. Leaders should offer workshops, seminars, and resources that help employees understand and practice compassionate leadership. This can include training on empathy, active listening, and emotional intelligence. By providing these resources, leaders can create a culture of care and empathy.

Reflective Exercise:

Reflect on how you currently lead with compassion within your team. Are there areas where you can improve? Write down specific actions you can take to enhance your compassionate leadership skills. Share these reflections with your team and develop a plan to implement them.

Principle 25: Sustain Momentum

Sustaining momentum involves continuously striving to maintain energy, enthusiasm, and a forward-thinking mindset within your team. When leaders sustain momentum, they ensure that the team remains motivated, engaged, and committed to achieving the organization's goals. This principle is crucial for driving long-term success and fostering a high-performing work environment.

"Success is not final, failure is not fatal: It is the courage to continue that counts."

— Winston Churchill

To sustain momentum, leaders should set clear and achievable goals that align with the organization's mission and vision. This means establishing specific, measurable, attainable, relevant, and time-bound (SMART) goals that provide direction and focus. Clear goals help to keep the team motivated and on track towards achieving the organization's objectives.

Providing regular updates and progress reports is crucial for sustaining momentum. Leaders should keep the team informed about the progress towards their goals and any changes or challenges that arise. This can include regular team meetings, emails, and newsletters. Regular updates help to maintain enthusiasm and ensure that everyone is aligned.

Recognizing and celebrating achievements is essential for reinforcing this principle. Leaders should acknowledge and reward the successes and milestones of the team, both big and small. This recognition helps to build a sense of pride and accomplishment, motivating employees to continue striving for excellence.

Encouraging continuous improvement and innovation is important for sustaining momentum. Leaders should create an environment where employees feel empowered to explore new ideas and take on new challenges. This involves supporting risk-taking, providing the necessary resources, and fostering a culture of creativity and innovation. Continuous improvement helps to keep the team engaged and motivated.

Providing opportunities for professional and personal development is crucial for sustaining momentum. Leaders should offer access to training, development, and career advancement opportunities that help employees grow and develop their skills. By investing in the growth of their team members, leaders can ensure that the team remains motivated and committed to achieving the organization's goals.

Reflective Exercise:

Reflect on how you currently sustain momentum within your team. Are there areas where you can improve? Write down specific actions you can take to enhance momentum. Share these reflections with your team and develop a plan to implement them.

Conclusion

As we reach the end of "*Compassionate Leadership: Building Strong Brands Through Empathy, Connection, and Continuous Improvement,*" it's clear that the journey of compassionate leadership is both profound and rewarding. This book has provided you with a comprehensive framework of principles and practical strategies to transform your leadership approach and, in turn, your organization. By embracing empathy, fostering genuine connections, and committing to continuous improvement, you have the tools to create a resilient and thriving brand.

"Compassionate leadership is about inspiring others to see their worth, nurturing their potential, and empowering them to lead with purpose and heart."

– Laura Templeton

Throughout this book, you have explored the core principles of compassionate leadership, reflected on your personal leadership style, and learned from the journey of Rebekah, a young leader navigating her new role. These insights are designed to be more than just theoretical knowledge; they are meant to be integrated into your daily practice, inspiring you to lead with authenticity and heart.

The 25 principles outlined in Part II serve as a robust reference guide, providing you with actionable insights and reflective exercises to deepen your understanding and application of compassionate leadership. Use these principles to guide your decisions, inspire your team, and create a culture where truth, trust, and talent are encouraged and celebrated.

However, the journey doesn't end here. The true impact of compassionate leadership is realized when these principles are brought to life within your organization. This requires ongoing commitment, reflection, and action. As a leader, you have the power to shape the future of your team and your brand, creating an environment where every individual feels valued, supported, and inspired to contribute their best.

Appendix

Additional Resources and Tools for Compassionate Leadership

Tools and Assessments:

1. Myers-Briggs Type Indicator (MBTI)
– A personality assessment tool that helps understand individual differences and improve teamwork.

2. StrengthsFinder 2.0 by Gallup
– An assessment tool to identify individual strengths and enhance team performance.

3. DiSC Profile
– A behavioral assessment tool that provides insights into communication styles and team dynamics.

4. Emotional Intelligence 2.0 by Travis Bradberry and Jean Greaves
– An assessment and training tool for developing emotional intelligence skills.

5. Harvard Business Review's Leadership Self-Assessment
– A self-assessment tool to evaluate and improve leadership capabilities.

Technology and AI Tools:

1. Slack: Team Collaboration Tool
– A platform for team communication and collaboration, enhancing transparency and efficiency.

2. Trello: Project Management Tool
– A tool for organizing tasks, projects, and workflows, fostering collaboration and productivity.

3. Zoom: Video Conferencing Tool
– A platform for virtual meetings and webinars, facilitating remote communication and collaboration.

4. ChatGPT by OpenAI: AI Communication Assistant
– Generates content, refines messaging, and streamlines

communication for leaders and teams.

5. Canva: AI-Powered Design Tool

– Simplifies creating branded visuals and marketing materials with AI-driven design features.

<u>**Well-being and Mindfulness Resources:**</u>

1. Headspace: Meditation and Mindfulness App

– A tool for promoting mental well-being and mindfulness in the workplace.

2. Calm: Meditation and Relaxation App

– An app offering guided meditations, sleep stories, and relaxation techniques.

3. The Happiness Project by Gretchen Rubin

– A book and resources focused on creating happiness and well-being in everyday life.

4. Workplace Wellness Programs: Wellness Council of America (WELCOA)

– Resources and programs for promoting wellness in the workplace.

5. The Resilience Institute: Resilience Training

– Training programs focused on building resilience and well-being for individuals and teams.

<u>**Additional Resources:**</u>

1. TED Talks: Leadership and Personal Development

– Inspirational talks on leadership, personal growth, and innovation.

2. Simon Sinek's "Start With Why" TED Talk

– A talk on the importance of finding and communicating your purpose.

3. Brené Brown's "The Power of Vulnerability" TED Talk

– A talk on the value of vulnerability and authenticity in leadership.

4. HBR Ascend: Articles and Resources for Emerging Leaders

– A collection of articles, videos, and resources for developing leadership skills.

5. Mind Tools: Leadership Skills Toolkit
– A comprehensive toolkit of resources and tools for developing leadership capabilities.

These resources and tools can support your journey toward compassionate leadership, providing valuable insights, practical strategies, and opportunities for continuous learning and improvement.

Invitation to Continue the Journey

To further support you on this transformative journey, I invite you to schedule a call to learn more about my workshops and development programs designed specifically for leaders and their teams. These workshops provide a hands-on, interactive experience that deepens the understanding and application of the principles discussed in this book. Whether you are looking to enhance your personal leadership skills or develop a comprehensive training program for your team, these workshops offer practical strategies and tailored support to help you achieve your goals.

By investing in compassionate leadership development, you are making a commitment to foster a positive, value-driven culture that will drive lasting success for your organization. Together, we can create a thriving, resilient brand that stands the test of time.

Thank you for embarking on this journey with me. Your dedication to compassionate leadership has the potential to create a ripple effect of positive change, extending far beyond the workplace. Let's continue this journey together, empowering each other to lead with empathy, connection, and a relentless commitment to continuous improvement.

With gratitude and encouragement,
Laura T.
Schedule a Call TODAY!

To learn more about how our workshops and development programs can benefit your organization, visit https://30SecondSuccess.com

Let's work together to build a brighter, more compassionate future for your team and your brand.

Acknowledgements

To my Lord and Savior, Jesus Christ, whose wisdom and guidance light my path and whose unwavering love gives me the courage to lead with purpose and compassion.

To my beloved husband, whose unwavering support and belief in me have been my anchor through every challenge and celebration. Your love and strength have turned dreams into reality and made every step of this journey possible.

To my children and grandchildren: Your love, joy, and boundless potential inspire me every day. You are a constant reminder to live by faith, share happiness, and strive to leave a legacy that matters.

To my loving parents—my father, whose memory continues to inspire me, and my mother, whose strength, encouragement, and faith guide me still—you have shaped me into the woman I am today. Your love and guidance remain my anchor.

To my good friend and confidant, Kristy Crippen, whose unwavering belief in me and wise counsel have been a source of strength and clarity. Your friendship has enriched my journey in countless ways.

And to all the remarkable individuals who have walked alongside me, encouraging me to pursue my dreams and never give up. This book is for you, and for all the leaders who strive to make a positive impact in the world, building teams and brands that thrive through compassion, connection, and purpose.

About the Author

Laura Templeton, affectionately known as *"Laura T.,"* is a leading authority on brand communication, branding with AI, and workplace advocacy. As the Founder and Chief Instigator of 30 Second Success, Laura has dedicated her career to empowering leaders, business owners, and professionals to refine their messaging, amplify their impact, and create lasting connections.

With over 25 years of experience in marketing and brand strategy, Laura's expertise is rooted in a solid corporate foundation, including tenures at RCA and a prestigious bank in New Jersey. Her strategic vision and ability to foster cohesive, high-performing teams have earned her a reputation as a trusted leader and innovator.

As a Heroic Public Speaking graduate who trained with Michael and Amy Port, Laura is a professionally trained speaker who captivates audiences with her dynamic and insightful presentations. She is a member of the National Speakers Association (NSA), Women Speakers Association (WSA), and 500Speakers, delivering impactful keynotes and workshops to organizations such as AmeriGas, Wells Fargo Advisors, TruMark Financial Credit Union, OnDoc, Sipology, the National Association of Women in Construction, Ellevate Network, Coaching Empire, Connected Leaders Academy, and esteemed academic institutions like Penn State University, Rowan College, and Bucks County Community College.

Laura's thought leadership extends to top media outlets. She has been featured in Thrive Global, the Harvard Book Store, and on renowned podcasts including Time to Shine Today, Women Winning Their Way, and Get Authentic with Marques Ogden. She is also the acclaimed author of *30 Second Success: Ditch the Pitch & Start Connecting!* and *Stand In Your Brand: Harness the Power of AI for Brand Success, Efficiency, and Client Attraction*. Her newest book, *Compassionate Leadership: Building Strong Brands Through Empathy, Connection, and Continuous Improvement*, inspires leaders to foster resilient, value-driven organizations.

Through her workshops, speaking engagements, and writing, Laura equips leaders and teams with the tools to connect authentically, embrace innovation, and lead with compassion. Based in Bradenton, Florida, Laura enjoys life with her supportive husband, her children and grandchildren, and her faithful office companion, Knox.

COMPASSIONATE LEADERSHIP 30 DAY CHALLENGE

Special **FREE** Bonus Gift for **YOU**!

Your Exclusive Companion to *Compassionate Leadership is HERE!*

Transform your leadership style one day at a time with the **30-Day Leadership Challenge**—a powerful, step-by-step guide to implementing the principles of compassionate leadership in your daily practice. This bonus resource is designed to help you build stronger connections, foster trust, and inspire your team to achieve greater success.

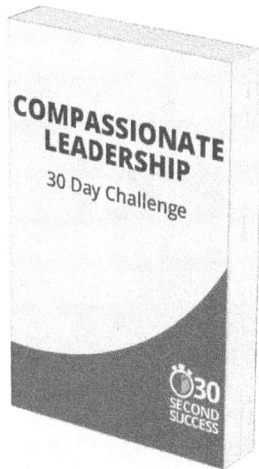

Get Your FREE e-Book And Over the Next 30 Days, You'll:

- **Master Core Leadership Principles:** Engage with daily prompts and activities that align with the book's key themes of empathy, connection, and continuous improvement.
- **Inspire Your Team:** Learn actionable strategies to foster collaboration, innovation, and purpose within your team.

- **Reflect and Grow:** Use guided exercises to deepen your understanding of compassionate leadership and identify areas for personal and professional development.
- **Build Lasting Habits:** Develop consistent practices that enhance your leadership impact over the long term.

Get your FREE e-Book HERE https://compassionate-leadership-book.com/challenge

THE IDEAL PROFESSIONAL SPEAKER FOR YOUR NEXT EVENT

If your organization is committed to developing strong, effective leaders and elevating your brand's visibility, book Laura Templeton for a keynote or workshop. As a dynamic speaker and author of *Compassionate Leadership*, Laura inspires teams to lead with clarity, confidence, and connection – fostering a culture of trust, impact, and lasting success. Secure your spot today!

TO CONTACT OR BOOK LAURA TO SPEAK:

30 Second Success

+1 (941) 297-3311

LauraTSpeaks.com

info@30SecondSuccess.com

Compassionate Leadership

"Share This Book"

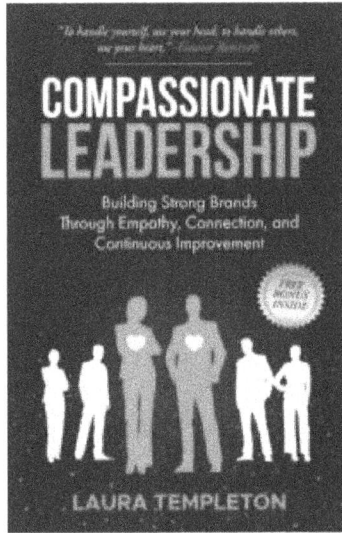

Retail $19.99 USD

Special Quantity Discounts

5-20 Books	17.99
21-99 Books	15.99
100-499 Books	13.99
500-999 Books	11.99
1000+ Books	9.99

*Price per book plus tax and shipping.

Other Books by the Author

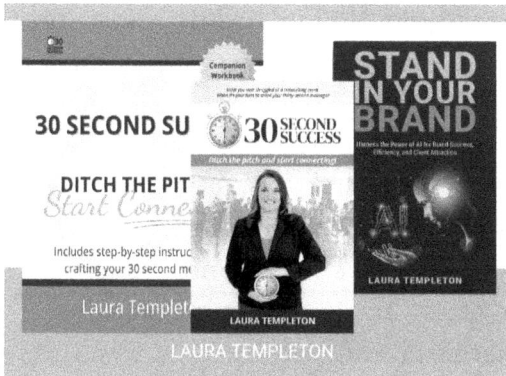

"30 Second Success: Ditch the Pitch and Start Connecting!" is a game-changing guide for professionals seeking to make lasting impressions in just 30 seconds. This book helps you move beyond outdated elevator pitches by teaching you how to craft authentic, engaging messages that resonate with your audience. Packed with actionable tips and real-world examples, it empowers you to build stronger connections, showcase your unique value, and attract the clients and opportunities you want. Whether you're networking, presenting, or meeting potential clients, this book will help you communicate with clarity, confidence, and purpose.

"30 Second Success: Ditch the Pitch and Start Connecting!" Companion Workbook is designed to compliment the bestselling book *30 Second Success: Ditch the Pitch and Start Connecting!*, this workbook is your step-by-step guide to crafting a 30-second message that grabs attention and inspires action. Perfect for networking events, client pitches, or everyday

conversations, this practical tool helps you create a message that makes every second count.

"Stand In Your Brand: *Harness the Power of AI for Brand Success, Efficiency and Client Attraction"* is an essential resource for professionals and entrepreneurs ready to elevate their brand with cutting-edge AI tools. This book g uides you through leveraging AI to clarify your brand message, streamline processes, and create impactful marketing strategies that attract your ideal clients. With practical insights and innovative approaches, it demystifies AI, showing you how to use it effectively while maintaining a human touch. Perfect for those looking to save time, increase efficiency, and stand out in a competitive marketplace, this book is your roadmap to building a powerful, authentic brand.

Discover how to elevate your brand and communication strategies with these great books! To learn more, visit 30secondsuccess.com/books and find out where to order your copy or receive a free copy, just by covering the shipping.

Take the first step to connectingwith clarity, confidence, and compassion today!

www.ingramcontent.com/pod-product-compliance
Lightning Source LLC
Chambersburg PA
CBHW052135270326
41930CB00012B/2898